THE FLY

and Other Horror Stories

Science is both our friend and our enemy. It invents medicines and electronic wheelchairs; it invents chemical weapons and bombs. But who can stop the march of science? Scientists will go on looking, thinking, exploring, wondering, inventing . . . and mistakes will be made, as they always have been.

A French professor in his laboratory works night and day on his new invention – a method of travelling that requires no actual movement at all. His research is nearly finished, his machines are ready, and now the experiments begin . . . with terrifying results. But horror in these stories is found not only in the laboratories of scientists. It is also found in a Californian desert town, in a mist on the Pacific, in an English cathedral, in a seaside town, on a London street, in the neat little house of a dear old lady. But most of all, horror lies in the mind, in those dark shadowy unexplored places in our memories and our dreams.

But we begin in France with a telephone call in the middle of the night – a woman phoning her brother-in-law with the most dreadful news . . .

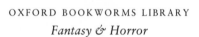

OXFORD BOOKWORMS LIBRARY

Fantasy & Horror

The Fly
and Other Horror Stories

Stage 6 (2500 headwords)

Series Editor: Jennifer Bassett
Founder Editor: Tricia Hedge
Activities Editors: Jennifer Bassett and Christine Lindop

RETOLD BY JOHN ESCOTT

The Fly

and Other Horror Stories

OXFORD UNIVERSITY PRESS

OXFORD
UNIVERSITY PRESS

Great Clarendon Street, Oxford OX2 6DP

Oxford University Press is a department of the University of Oxford.
It furthers the University's objective of excellence in research, scholarship,
and education by publishing worldwide in

Oxford New York

Auckland Cape Town Dar es Salaam Hong Kong Karachi
Kuala Lumpur Madrid Melbourne Mexico City Nairobi
New Delhi Shanghai Taipei Toronto

With offices in

Argentina Austria Brazil Chile Czech Republic France Greece
Guatemala Hungary Italy Japan Poland Portugal Singapore
South Korea Switzerland Thailand Turkey Ukraine Vietnam

This simplified edition © Oxford University Press 2008

Database right Oxford University Press (maker)

First published in Oxford Bookworms 2003

8 10 9 7

No unauthorized photocopying

ISBN 978 0 19 479261 5

Printed in China

ACKNOWLEDGEMENTS
Illustrations by: David A. Roach

Word count (main text): 28,930 words

For more information on the Oxford Bookworms Library,
visit www.oup.com/bookworms

CONTENTS

ACKNOWLEDGEMENTS

The publishers are grateful to the following for their kind permission to adapt copyright material:

• Artellus Limited on behalf of the Estate of Robert Aickman for *Ringing the Changes* by Robert Aickman;
• David Higham Associates for *The Landlady* by Roald Dahl from *Kiss Kiss*, first published in Great Britain in 1960 by Michael Joseph Ltd, copyright © Roald Dahl 1959.
• Watson, Little Limited for *Cooking the Books* by Christopher Fowler;
• Mrs Joan Temple for *The Whispering Gallery* by William F. Temple;
• A. P. Watt Limited on behalf of the Literary Executors of the Estate of H. G. Wells for *The Stolen Body* by H. G. Wells, from *The Complete Stories of H. G. Wells*.

The publishers have made every effort to contact the copyright holder for *The Fly* by George Langelaan, but have been unable to do so. If the copyright holder would like to contact the publishers, the publishers would be happy to pay an appropriate adaptation fee.

The Fly

George Langelaan

The sound of a telephone ringing has always made me uneasy. I have never liked telephones, and here in France we now have so many of them that you are never safe from interruption. The worst thing is when the telephone rings in the dead of night. If anyone could see me turn on the light to answer it, I suppose I would look like any other sleepy man annoyed at being disturbed. But the truth is that I am fighting down the feeling that a stranger has broken into the house and is in my bedroom. I only get back to a more normal state when I recognize the voice at the other end and when I know what is wanted of me.

However, I had become expert at overcoming this fear and had trained myself to speak calmly, no matter what was said to me. So when my sister-in-law phoned at two in the morning, asking me to come over, but first to warn the police that she had just killed my brother, I spoke in my usual calm manner.

'How have you killed André? Why?'

'But François! . . . I can't explain all that over the telephone. Please call the police and come quickly.'

'Maybe I had better see you first, Hélène?' I said.

'No, call the police first, or they'll ask you awkward questions. They'll have enough trouble believing that I did it alone . . . And I suppose you ought to tell them that André . . . André's body, is down at the factory . . . under the steam hammer.'

'He's *where?*'

'Under the steam hammer! Please come quickly, François! I can't bear it much longer!'

Have you ever tried to explain to a sleepy police officer that your sister-in-law has just phoned to say she has killed your brother with a steam hammer?

'Yes, Monsieur, I hear you . . . but who are you? What is your name? Where do you live? I said, where do you live!'

It was then that Commissaire Charas took the phone. He at least seemed to understand what I said, and told me he would pick me up and take me to my brother's house.

I had just managed to pull on trousers and a shirt and grab a hat and coat, when a black Citroën stopped outside the door.

'I assume you have a night watchman at your factory, Monsieur Delambre. Has he called you?' asked Commissaire Charas, as I got into the car.

'No, he hasn't,' I said. 'Though of course my brother could have entered the factory through the laboratory. He often works there late at night . . . all night, sometimes.'

'Your brother is a professor, yes? Is his work connected with your business?'

'No, my brother is, or was, doing research work for the Air Ministry. He wanted to be away from Paris but near skilled workmen who could build things for his experiments, so I offered him one of the old workshops of the factory. He lives in our grandfather's old house on the hill behind the factory.'

'What sort of research work?'

'He rarely talked about it. I suppose the Air Ministry could tell you. I only know that he was about to start experiments he had been preparing for some months. Something to do with the disintegration of solid objects, he told me.'

2

The commissaire drove through the open factory gate, stopped by the main entrance, and we got out of the car. A policeman stepped out of the doorway and led us to one of the workshops where all the lights were on. More policemen were standing by the steam hammer, watching two men with a camera. The camera was pointing downwards, and I made an effort to look.

My brother lay flat on his stomach across the conveyor line which carried the white-hot pieces of metal up to the hammer. The hammer was in its fully lowered position, and I saw that André's head and arm could only be a flattened mess.

The commissaire turned to me. 'How can we raise the hammer, Monsieur Delambre?'

'I'll raise it for you.'

'Would you like us to get one of your men to do it?'

'No, I'll be all right. The controls are just here. It was originally a steam hammer, but everything is worked electrically now. Look, the hammer is set at 50 tons, and the drop at zero. One thing I am sure of: my brother's wife certainly did not know how to set and operate this hammer.'

'Perhaps it was set that way last night when work stopped.'

'No,' I said. 'The drop is never set at zero.'

'I see. May I do it? It won't be very nice to watch, you know.'

'No, I'll be all right.'

Watching my brother's back, I pushed the switch and the steel hammer shook slightly, then rose quickly. As André's body was released, the trapped blood poured all over the horrible mess revealed under the hammer.

I turned and was violently sick in front of a young policeman, whose face was as green as mine must have been.

◨ ◨ ◨

For weeks afterwards, Commissaire Charas investigated my brother's death. Later, we became quite friendly and he admitted that, for a long time, he had suspected me of killing André. But he could find no evidence and no motive.

Hélène was so calm during the investigation that the doctors finally decided she was mad (something I had for a long time thought the only possible solution), so there was no trial. She never tried to defend herself and even got quite annoyed when she realized people thought she *was* mad. This of course was considered proof that she was mad. She confessed to the murder of her husband and proved easily that she knew how to work the steam hammer. But she would never say why or under what circumstances she had killed André. The great mystery was why my brother had so helpfully put his head under the hammer – the only possible explanation for his part in that night's events.

The night watchman had heard the hammer twice. This was very strange because Hélène insisted that she had only used it once. But this seemed to be just another proof of her madness.

Commissaire Charas at first wondered if the victim really was my brother. But there was no possible doubt because the fingerprints of his left hand were the same as those found all over his laboratory and up at the house.

Six people from the Air Ministry came to the laboratory and went through all his papers. They took away some of his instruments, but told the commissaire that the most interesting documents and instruments had been destroyed.

The police laboratory at Lyons reported that André's head had been wrapped in a piece of velvet when it was smashed by the hammer. It was the brown velvet cloth I had seen on a table in my brother's laboratory.

After a few days in prison, Hélène had been moved to a nearby asylum for the criminally insane. Henri, Hélène and André's son, came to live with me. He was six years old.

Hélène was allowed visitors at the asylum, and I went to see her on Sundays. Once or twice the commissaire accompanied me and later I learned that he had also visited Hélène alone. But we were never able to obtain any information from my sister-in-law. She rarely answered questions and spent a lot of her time sewing, but her favourite activity seemed to be catching flies, which she always released unharmed after examining them carefully.

Only once was Hélène's behaviour so wild and uncontrollable that the doctor had to give her a powerful drug to calm her down. It was the day she saw a nurse killing flies.

The day after this, Commissaire Charas came to see me.

'I have a strange feeling that this business with the flies holds the answer to the whole mystery, Monsieur Delambre,' he said.

'But why?' I said. 'Isn't my poor sister-in-law's extreme interest in flies just one sign of her madness?'

'Do you believe she is really mad?'

'My dear Commissaire, how can there be any doubt?'

'I believe Madame Delambre has a very clear brain . . . even when catching flies.'

'But how do you explain her attitude towards her little boy?' I asked. 'She never seems to consider him as her own child.'

'I have thought about that, Monsieur Delambre. She may be trying to protect him. Perhaps she fears the boy, or even hates him. We don't know.'

'I'm afraid I don't understand, Commissaire.'

'Have you noticed that she never catches flies when the boy is there?' he said.

5

Hélène's favourite activity seemed to be catching flies.

'No. But now I think about it, you're quite right. Yes, that is strange . . . But I still don't understand.'

'Nor do I, Monsieur Delambre. And I'm very much afraid we shall never understand, unless perhaps your sister-in-law should . . . get better.'

'The doctors seem to think there is no hope of that,' I said.

'Do you know if your brother ever did any experiments with flies?'

'I really don't know, but I shouldn't think so. Have you asked the Air Ministry people? They knew all about the work.'

'Yes, and they laughed at me.'

'I can understand that,' I said.

'You are very fortunate to understand anything, Monsieur Delambre,' he said. 'I do not . . . but I hope to some day.'

◧ ◧ ◧

'Tell me, Uncle, do flies live a long time?'

We were just finishing our lunch and I was pouring some wine into Henri's glass for him to dip a biscuit in. It was lucky that he was staring at the wine glass and not at me, or something in my expression might have frightened him.

This was the first time he had ever mentioned flies, and I was relieved that Commissaire Charas was not present. I could imagine how eagerly he would question the boy.

'I don't know, Henri. Why do you ask?' I said cautiously.

'Because I have again seen the fly that Mama was looking for.'

'I didn't know your mother was looking for a fly,' I said.

'Yes, she was. It has grown quite a lot, but I recognized it all right.'

'Where did you see this fly, Henri, and . . . how did you recognize it?'

'This morning, on your desk, Uncle François. Its head is white instead of black, and it has a strange sort of leg.'

Feeling more and more like Commissaire Charas, but trying to look unconcerned, I went on:

'And when did you see this fly for the first time?'

'The day that Papa went away. I had caught it, but Mama made me let it go. Afterwards, she changed her mind and wanted me to find it again.'

'I think that fly must have died long ago, Henri,' I said, getting up and walking to the door.

But as soon as I was out of the room, I ran up the stairs to my study. There was no fly to be seen anywhere.

I was worried. Henri had just proved that Charas seemed to be getting close to some kind of clue in this business with the flies.

Did Charas know more than he was saying? I wondered. And for the first time, I also wondered about Hélène. Was she really insane? I had a strange, horrible feeling that somehow Charas was right – Hélène *was getting away with it!*

What could be the reason for such a terrible crime? What had led up to it? Just exactly what had happened?

I thought of all the hundreds of questions that Charas had asked Hélène. She had answered very few, always in a calm quiet voice. She had seemed perfectly sane then.

Charas was more than just an intelligent and educated police officer. He had an amazing ability to detect a lie even before it was spoken. I knew that he had believed the answers Hélène had given him. But then there were all the questions she had never answered: the most important ones.

She had been very willing to speak about her life with my brother – which seemed a happy and ordinary one – up to the time he died. About his death, however, she would say nothing more than that she had killed him with the steam hammer. She refused to say why, or how she had got my brother to put his head under it.

'I cannot answer that question,' was all she would reply.

Hélène, as I have said, had shown the commissaire that she knew how to operate the steam hammer. But she would not explain why it had been used *twice*. Finally, she had admitted:

'All right, I lied to you. I did use the hammer twice. But don't ask me why, because I cannot tell you.'

'And is that your only lie, Madame Delambre?' asked the commissaire.

'It is . . . and you know it,' was her reply.

I had thought about going to see the commissaire, but knowing that he would then start questioning Henri made me hesitate. I was also afraid that he would look for and find the fly Henri had talked of. And that annoyed me, because I could find no satisfactory explanation for that particular fear.

André had not been the absent-minded sort of professor. He enjoyed life, had a good sense of humour, loved children and animals, and could not bear to see anyone suffer.

What, then, could have made him put his head under that hammer? There were only two possible explanations. Either he had gone mad, or else he had a reason for letting his wife kill him in such a strange and terrible way.

I decided I would try to question Hélène myself.

When I arrived at the asylum that afternoon, Hélène took me outside. 'Let me show you my garden,' she said.

She was allowed to go into the garden during certain hours of the day, and had been given a little square where she could grow flowers. I had sent her seeds and some rose bushes out of my garden.

She took me to a seat near her little square of ground.

'François, I want to ask you something,' she said. 'Do flies live a long time?'

Staring at her, I was about to say that her boy had asked the very same question a few hours earlier. Instead, I decided to try a sudden attack.

'I don't really know, Hélène; but the fly you were looking for was in my study this morning.'

She turned her head round with such force that I heard the bones crack in her neck. She opened her mouth, but said nothing; only her eyes seemed to be screaming with fear.

I had broken through her defences . . . but to what? The commissaire would have known what to do with such an advantage; I did not. All I could do was hope that those defences would continue to break down.

She put both her hands over her open mouth. 'François . . . did you kill it?' she whispered, her eyes searching my face.

'No.'

'You have it then . . . you have it with you! Give it to me!' she almost shouted, seizing my arm with both her hands.

'No, Hélène, I haven't got it.'

'But you know now . . . you've guessed, haven't you?'

'No, Hélène. I only know one thing, and that is that you are not insane. But I intend to know everything, Hélène, and either you tell me and I'll see what is to be done, or . . .'

'Or what? Say it!'

'Or your friend the commissaire will have that fly first thing tomorrow morning.'

She remained quite still, looking down at her hands. 'If I tell you . . . will you promise to destroy that fly before doing anything else?'

'No, Hélène. I can make no promises until I know everything.'

'But François, you must understand. I promised André that fly would be destroyed, and I can say nothing until it is.'

'Hélène, as soon as the police examine that fly they will know that you are not insane, and then . . .'

'François, no! For Henri's <u>sake</u>! Don't you see? I was expecting that fly. I was hoping it would find me, but it couldn't know that I was here. What else could it do but go to others it loves, to Henri, to you – you who might know and understand what needed to be done!'

Was she really mad, or was she pretending again? 'Tell me everything, Hélène,' I said. 'Then I can protect your boy.'

'Protect my boy from what? Don't you understand? I'm here so that Henri won't be the son of a woman who went to the guillotine for having murdered his father! Don't you understand that I would much prefer the guillotine to the living death of this asylum?'

'I understand, Hélène, and I'll do my best for Henri whether you tell me or not. But if you don't, there'll be nothing more I can do, because Commissaire Charas will have the fly.'

'But why must you know?' she asked, almost angrily.

'Because I must and will know how and why my brother died,' I said.

'All right, take me back to the house,' she said. 'I'll give you what your commissaire would call my "confession".'

I took her back and waited while she went up to her room. She came back some minutes later with a large brown envelope.

'All I ask is that you read this alone,' she said. 'After that, you may do as you wish.'

'I'll read it tonight,' I said, taking the precious envelope. 'I'll come and see you again tomorrow.'

'Just as you like,' said my sister-in-law. She went back upstairs without saying goodbye.

▣ ▣ ▣

When I was at home, I read the words on the envelope:

TO WHOM IT MAY CONCERN
(probably Commissaire Charas)

I told the servants that I would have only a light supper and that I was not to be disturbed afterwards. I ran upstairs, threw Hélène's envelope onto my desk and made another careful search of the room. There was no fly.

When the servant brought my supper, I poured myself a glass of wine, and locked the door after her. I then disconnected the telephone – I always did this now at night – and turned out all the lights except the lamp on my desk.

I opened Hélène's envelope and took out several closely written pages. The first page contained these words:

This is not a confession because, although I killed my husband, I am not a murderer. I simply and faithfully carried out his last wish by smashing his head and right arm under the steam hammer of his brother's factory.

I turned the page and began to read.

▣ ▣ ▣

For a year before his death, my husband had told me about some of his experiments. He knew that the Air Ministry would have forbidden some of them as too dangerous, but he wanted to be certain about the results before reporting his discovery.

André claimed to have discovered a way of transmitting solid objects through space. Any solid object placed in his 'transmitter' was instantly disintegrated – and then reintegrated in a special receiving machine.

André believed that his transmitter was the most important discovery since the invention of the wheel. He believed it would change life as we know it. It would mean the end of all ways of moving things from one place to another – not only things but also people. He could see a time when there would be no aeroplanes, ships, trains or cars and, therefore, no roads or railway lines, ports, airports or stations. They would be replaced all over the world by stations for transmitting and receiving objects. A traveller would be placed in a cabin at the station, the machine would be turned on, and the traveller would disappear and reappear almost immediately at the chosen receiving station.

André's receiving machine was only a few feet away from his transmitter, in the next room of his laboratory. His first successful experiment was with an ashtray. It was the first time he told me about his experiments and he came running into the house and threw the ashtray into my hands.

'Hélène, look!' he cried. 'For one ten-millionth of a second, that ashtray has been completely disintegrated. For one little moment it did not exist! It was only atoms travelling through space at the speed of light! A moment later, the atoms were once more gathered together in the shape of an ashtray!'

'André, please! What on earth are you talking about?'

He laughed. 'Do you remember I once told you about some mysterious flying stones in India? They come flying into houses as if thrown from outside, even though the doors and windows are closed.'

'Yes,' I said. 'And I remember your friend, Professor Augier, saying that the only possible explanation was that the stones had been disintegrated outside the house, had then come through the walls, and been reintegrated before hitting the floor or opposite walls. But I still don't understand how it is possible.'

'It's possible because the atoms that make up objects are not close together like the bricks of a wall. They are separated by the hugeness of space.'

'Are you saying that you have disintegrated that ashtray, then put it together again after pushing it through something?' I said.

'Yes, Hélène! I sent it through the wall that separates my transmitter from my receiving machine. Isn't it wonderful?'

'Yes, André. But don't ever transmit me. I'd be afraid of coming out at the other end like your ashtray.'

'What do you mean?' he asked.

'Do you remember what was written under that ashtray?'

'Yes, of course. "Made in Japan".'

'The words are still there, André, but . . . look!'

He took the ashtray out of my hands and looked at it. His face went quite pale. The three words were still there, but reversed:

napaJ ni edaM

Without a word, André rushed off to his laboratory. I only saw him the next morning, tired after a whole night's work.

A few days later, André had a new problem which made him fussy and bad-tempered for several weeks. One evening he apologized.

'I'm sorry, my dear,' he said. 'I've been working my way through many problems, and I haven't been very pleasant to live with. You see, my first experiment with a live animal was a complete disaster.'

14

'André! You tried that experiment with Dandelo, didn't you?'

'Yes,' he said, unhappily. 'He disintegrated perfectly, but he never reappeared in the receiving machine. There is no more Dandelo, only the atoms of a cat wandering somewhere in space.'

Dandelo was a small white cat who had come into our garden one day and remained with us. I had wondered where it had gone lately. I was quite angry, but my husband was so miserable that I said nothing.

I saw little of him during the next few weeks. He had most of his meals in the laboratory. Then one evening he came home smiling, and I knew that his troubles were over.

'I've got everything perfect at last!' he said. 'And I want you to be the first to see it happen.'

'Wonderful, André!' I said. 'I'll be delighted.'

We had a special dinner to celebrate and at the end of the meal, when the servant brought in the bottle of champagne, André took it from her.

'We'll celebrate with reintegrated champagne!' he said, leading the way down to the laboratory.

I held the champagne and glasses while he unlocked the door and switched on the lights. He then opened the door of a telephone booth he had bought, and which he had made into his transmitter. He put a chair inside the booth, then said:

'Put the bottle down on that.'

Having carefully closed the door, he took me to the other end of the room and gave me a pair of very dark sun glasses. He put on another pair and walked back to the booth.

'Don't take your glasses off until I tell you,' he said.

Then he pushed a switch and the whole room was brightly lit

15

by an orange flash of light. I saw a ball of fire inside the transmitter and felt its heat on my face and hands. The whole thing lasted less than a second.

'Now you can take off your glasses, Hélène,' André said.

He opened the door of the booth – and I was amazed to see that the bottle of champagne and the chair were not there.

André then took me into the next room. There was a second telephone booth in the corner. Opening the door, he lifted the bottle of champagne off the chair.

'Are you sure it's not dangerous to drink?' I asked, as he opened the bottle.

'Absolutely sure, Hélène,' he said, giving me a glass. 'Drink this and I'll show you something much more amazing.'

We went back into the other room.

'Oh, André!' I said. 'Remember poor Dandelo!'

'This is only a guinea pig, Hélène. But I'm certain it will go through all right.'

He put the little animal on the floor of the booth and quickly closed the door. I put on my dark glasses again and saw and felt the ball of fire.

Without waiting for André, I rushed into the next room and looked into the receiving booth.

'Oh, André, he's there!' I shouted. 'You've succeeded!'

'I hope so,' he said. 'If this little animal is still alive and well in a month, we can then consider the experiment a success.'

That month of waiting seemed like a year. And then one day André put Miquette, our dog, into his 'transmitter'. He did not tell me first, knowing very well that I would never have agreed to such an experiment with our dog. When he did tell me, Miquette had been successfully transmitted five or six times.

16

'She seemed to enjoy the experience,' André said.

I now expected that my husband would invite the Air Ministry people to come down, but he went on working.

'There are some parts I do not yet fully understand myself,' he said. 'I must be able to explain how and why it works.'

Of course I never thought that he would try an experiment with a human being, not then anyway. It was only after the accident that I discovered he had put a second set of the control switches inside the disintegration booth, so that he could use himself as the object of the experiment.

The morning André tried this terrible experiment, he did not come home for lunch. I sent the servant down with some food, but she brought it back with a note she had found outside the laboratory door: DO NOT DISTURB ME, I AM WORKING.

It was just a little later when Henri came running into the room to say that he had caught a funny fly. Refusing even to look at his closed hand, I ordered him to release it immediately.

'But it has such a funny white head!' he said.

I took him to the open window and ordered him to release the fly. I knew that Henri had caught the fly because it looked different from other flies, but I also knew that his father hated cruelty to animals and that there would be a fuss if he discovered our son had put a fly in a box or bottle.

At dinner time that evening I had still not seen André, so I ran down to the laboratory and knocked at the door. He did not answer, but I heard him moving around. A moment later he pushed a note under the door. It was typewritten:

Hélène, I am having trouble. Put the boy to bed and come back in an hour's time.

I went back to the house and put Henri to bed, then I returned to the laboratory where I found another note pushed under the door. My hand shook as I picked it up because I knew by then that something must be terribly wrong. I read:

Hélène, first of all I rely on you to be brave, because you alone can help me. I have had a serious accident. It is useless talking to me, because I cannot answer, I cannot speak. Please do exactly what I ask. Knock three times on the door to show that you understand, and then fetch me a bowl of milk with some brandy in it.

Shaking with fear, I did as he asked, and in less than five minutes I was back. There was another note under the door.

Hélène, when you knock, I'll open the door. Walk over to my desk and put down the bowl of milk. Then go into the other room where the receiving booth is. Look carefully and try to find a fly which ought to be there, but which I am unable to find. Unfortunately I cannot see small things very easily.

Promise not to look at me or talk to me. I cannot answer you. Knock again three times and I will know I have your promise. My life depends on the help you give me.

I had to calm myself before I knocked slowly three times. I heard André moving behind the door, then it opened. Out of the corner of my eye, I saw that he was standing behind the door. Without looking round, I carried the bowl of milk to his desk.

'My dear, you can rely on me,' I said gently. I put the bowl on his desk, then walked into the next room where all the lights were on.

There were papers everywhere, chairs lay on their sides, and one of the window curtains was half-torn and hanging down. And in the fireplace there was a heap of burned documents.

I knew I would not find the fly André wanted me to look for.

18

Women know things that can't be explained by reason; this kind of knowledge is rarely understood by men. I already knew that the fly André wanted was the one which Henri had caught and which I had made him release.

I heard André moving in the next room, and then a strange sucking noise, as though he had trouble drinking his milk.

'André, there is no fly here,' I said, trying to speak calmly. 'Can you help me? Knock once for yes, twice for no.'

He knocked twice for 'no'.

'May I come to you?' I said. 'I don't know what has happened, my love, but I promise to be brave.'

After a moment of hesitation, he knocked once on his desk.

I stopped at the door, horrified. André had his head and shoulders covered by the brown velvet cloth from the table.

'André, we'll make a thorough search tomorrow,' I said. 'Why don't you go to bed? I'll take you to the guest room. I won't let anybody see you.'

His left hand knocked the desk twice.

'Do you need a doctor, André?' I asked.

'No,' he knocked, quickly.

I did not know what to do or say. And then I said, 'Henri caught a fly this morning, but I made him release it. He said its head was white. Could it be the one you're looking for?'

André let out a strange sigh and let his right arm drop. Instead of his hand, a grey stick like the branch of a tree hung out of his sleeve, almost down to his knee.

I had to bite my fingers to stop myself screaming. 'André, my love, tell me what happened. André . . . Oh, it's terrible!'

He knocked once for yes, then pointed to the door. I went out and sank down to the floor crying as he locked the door behind

André let out a strange sigh and let his right arm drop.

me. He started typing again and I waited. At last he came to the door and pushed a note under it.

Hélène, come back in the morning. I must think and by then I will have typed out an explanation for you. Take one of my sleeping pills and go to bed. I need you fresh and strong tomorrow, my poor love.

□ □ □

20

Because of the sleeping pill I slept heavily, without dreaming. I woke suddenly at 7 a.m., ran down to the kitchen, and prepared coffee, bread and butter.

André opened the laboratory door as soon as I knocked and I took in the food. His head was still covered, and on his desk lay a typewritten sheet of paper, which I picked up. André pointed to the other door, and I walked into the next room. He shut the door after me, and I heard him pouring out coffee as I read:

You remember the ashtray experiment? I have had a similar accident. I 'transmitted' myself successfully the night before last. During a second experiment yesterday, a fly must have got into the 'disintegrator'. My only hope is to find that fly and take it through with me again. Please search for it carefully. If it is not found, I shall have to find a way to put an end to all this.

I cried softly, imagining some horrible re-arrangement of André's face – perhaps his eyes where his ears should be, or his mouth at the back of his neck. Or worse . . .

André must be saved! The fly must be found!

'André, may I come in?' I said.

He opened the door.

'André, don't despair. I'm going to find that fly. It can't be far away. But there must be no talk of "putting an end to all this". If you don't wish to be seen, I'll make you a mask until you get well again. If you cannot work, I'll call Professor Augier, and he and all your other friends will save you. Now, can't you let me see your face, André? I won't be afraid.'

But he knocked a 'no' on his desk and pointed to the door.

I will never forget that day-long hunt for a fly. I made all the servants join in the search. I told them a fly had escaped from the Professor's laboratory and that it must be caught alive. It was clear they thought I was crazy. They said so to the police later, and that hunt for a fly probably saved me from the guillotine.

I questioned Henri and frightened the poor boy by my wild, fierce manner. But then I kissed him and made him understand what I wanted. Yes, he remembered, he had found the fly by the kitchen window but had released it immediately as ordered.

I examined all the many flies we caught that day, but none had anything like a white head. That night, as I began to take André's dinner down to him, I stopped by the telephone. I had no doubt that André would kill himself unless I could make him change his mind. He would never forgive me for breaking a promise, but I phoned Professor Augier.

'The professor is away until the end of the week,' a polite voice at the other end informed me.

So I would have to fight alone. But I would save André.

I took the food down to the laboratory and, after he let me in, put it on his desk. Then I went into the next room.

'I want to know exactly what happened,' I said as he closed the door after me. 'Please tell me, André.'

He typed an answer and pushed it under the door.

Hélène, I do not want to tell you. Since I must leave you, I would rather you remembered me as I was before. I must destroy myself in such a way that nobody can possibly know what has happened to me. I have thought of a way which is neither simple nor easy, but you can and will help me.

'But why don't you tell the other professors about your discovery?' I said. 'They will help you and save you, André!'

Several furious knocks shook the door, and I knew then that he would never accept this solution. I talked to him for hours about me, about our boy, about his family, but he did not reply.

22

At last I cried, 'André, do you hear me?'

'Yes,' he knocked very gently.

'Listen. I have another idea. You remember the ashtray? Perhaps if you had put it through again, it might have come out with the letters turned back the right way.'

He was typing before I finished speaking.

I have already thought of that. It is why I wanted the fly. It must go through with me. There is no hope otherwise.

'Please try, André!' I said.

I have tried seven times already, but to please you I will try again. If you cannot find the dark glasses, turn away from the machine and put your hands over your eyes.

'I'm ready, André!' I shouted, turning and covering my eyes.

After what seemed a very long wait, but was probably only a minute or two, I saw a bright light through my fingers.

I turned round as the booth door opened.

His head and shoulders still covered with the velvet cloth, André stepped carefully out of the booth.

'Do you feel any different?' I asked, touching his arm.

He moved away quickly and fell over one of the chairs. As he fell, the velvet cloth slowly dropped off his head and shoulders.

The horror was too much for me. I screamed again and again but could not stop looking at him. And yet I knew that if I looked at the horror for much longer, I would go on screaming for the rest of my life.

Slowly, the monster, the thing that had been my husband, covered its head, got up and found its way into the other room.

I hope there is no life after death because, if there is, I shall never forget the horror! Day and night, awake or asleep, I see it, and I know that I will see it forever.

Nothing can ever make me forget that dreadful white hairy head with its two pointed ears. Pink and wet, the nose was also that of a cat, a huge cat. But the eyes! Where the eyes should have been, there were two brown shapes the size of saucers. Instead of a mouth there was a long hairy vertical cut. From this hung something long and black and wet at the end.

I must have fainted because I found myself on the floor of the laboratory, staring at the closed door. Behind it I could hear the noise of André's typewriter. Then the noise stopped and a sheet of paper came under the door. Trembling with fear and disgust, I crawled over to where I could read it without touching it.

Now you understand. The last experiment was a new disaster, my poor Hélène. I suppose you recognized part of Dandelo's head. When I went into the disintegrator, my head was only that of a fly. Now, only the eyes and mouth remain. The rest is part of a cat's head. You can see that there is only one solution. I must disappear. Knock on the door when you are ready and I will explain what you have to do.

Getting up, I went to the door and tried to speak. No sound came out of my throat, so I knocked once.

You can, of course, guess the rest. He explained his plan in short, typewritten notes, and I agreed to everything.

I followed him into the silent factory. In my hand was a page of explanations: what I had to know about the steam hammer. He pointed to the control switch as he went past, and I watched him stop in front of that terrible instrument.

I watched him kneel down, wrap a cloth round his head, and lie down flat on the floor.

It was not difficult. I was not killing my husband. André, poor André, had gone long ago, it seemed. Without hesitating, I pushed

24

the switch. The great metal hammer seemed to drop slowly. My husband . . . the thing's body shook for a second and then lay still.

It was then I noticed that he had forgotten to put his right arm – his fly leg – under the hammer. The police would never understand but the professors would, and they must not! That had been André's last wish.

I had to do it quickly. The night watchman must have heard the hammer and would be round at any moment. I pushed the other switch and the hammer slowly lifted. Seeing, but trying not to look, I ran forward and put the right arm under the hammer. Then I came back and pushed the first switch. The hammer came down a second time.

Then I ran all the way home.

You know the rest and can now do whatever you think right.

So ended Helen's 'confession'.

▣ ▣ ▣

The next day I telephoned Commissaire Charas to invite him to dinner. He arrived at eight o'clock that evening.

'You heard about my poor sister-in-law?' I said.

'Yes, soon after you telephoned me this morning,' he said. 'I am sorry, but perhaps it was for the best.'

'I suppose she killed herself.'

'Without a doubt,' he said. 'We found more of the fatal drug sewn into her dress.'

'I would like to show you a very strange document after dinner, Charas,' I said.

'Ah, yes. I heard that Madame Delambre had been writing a lot, but we could find nothing but the short note informing us that she was taking her own life.'

During our dinner, we talked about politics, books, films, and the local football club. After dinner I took him up to my study where there was a warm fire to sit by.

'I would like you to read this, Charas,' I said. 'First because it was partly intended for you, and secondly because it will interest you. I would like to burn it afterwards.'

Without a word, he took the sheets of paper Hélène had given me and started to read. Twenty minutes later he carefully folded them and put them into the brown envelope. Then he put the envelope into the fire.

When it was burning, he said, 'I think it proves beyond all doubt that Madame Delambre was quite insane.'

For a long time we watched the fire eating up Hélène's 'confession'.

'A strange thing happened to me this morning, Charas. I went to the cemetery where my brother's body is buried. It was quite empty and I was alone.'

'Not quite, Monsieur Delambre,' he said. 'I was there, but I did not want to disturb you.'

'Then you saw me . . .'

'Yes, I saw you bury a small box.'

'Do you know what was in it?'

'A fly, I suppose,' he said.

'Yes. I had found it early this morning, caught in a spider's web in the garden.'

'Was it dead?' he asked.

'No, not quite. I . . . killed it . . . between two stones. Its head was . . . white . . . all white.'

Cooking the Books

Christopher Fowler

Haldeman had left nothing to chance. When he stepped out of his office on Friday evening, he walked through the restaurant instead of going straight down to the garage. He stopped to talk for a few minutes with José and the head waiter, as if it were just the end of another quiet week.

On the way home he was surprised to find that he was sweating, even though it was quite cool inside the car. Haldeman looked at himself in the car mirror, and what he saw disturbed him. A forty-eight-year-old man whose once-round face had grown thin with worry, whose shirt collars were now two sizes too big. Even his wedding ring was loose on his finger. His suit fitted <u>badly</u> across his shoulders. It was years old, but how could he afford to buy a new one? When Mona left him, she said she would take every dollar of his money, but how could she take what he didn't have?

He stopped the Toyota in front of his apartment building. It was a beautiful evening. In Los Angeles the evenings were always beautiful, but this one also <u>held</u> the promise of escape.

Haldeman went up to his apartment where he mixed himself a drink and went over the details of his plan. The truth was, he was <u>facing</u> financial ruin. With each week that passed, the restaurant earned less and less. Who could say why? It had been a great idea, even Mona had agreed. With the small amount he had saved, and the money from Mona, he had managed to convince the bank to lend him an equal amount to start a restaurant specializing in barbecued food.

Each evening at five, 'Haldeman's', the blue and purple sign above the restaurant, lit up the Los Angeles sky. The position had seemed perfect, right on the corner of La Cienega and Santa Monica Boulevard. José, the chef, was excellent, the waiters were eager to please, yet something had gone wrong. The fashionable crowd had moved away to downtown restaurants, and without them to pay crazy prices, how could he hope to pay his bills? Add to that the money needed for his apartment, for his ex-wife Mona, for his gambling debts – yes, he had started gambling again – and you had the picture of a man moving fast towards disaster.

Haldeman finished his drink and went to the bedroom to pack. If he left soon, he would arrive in Palm Springs in time for a relaxing dinner at that new Japanese place on Highway 111. It shouldn't take him more than two and a half hours to drive there tonight. Nobody else would be going that way at this time of the year. He silently thanked the gods for sending him someone as stupid as Larry Hyatt. Silly, harmless, never-say-no Hyatt, who was about to play his part in a plan so simple and perfect that nothing – *nothing* – could possibly go wrong.

Haldeman loaded up the car and drove away from the apartment building. Already he was beginning to feel better, although he would not be able to celebrate until tomorrow evening, when he would arrive back in Los Angeles to find his restaurant burnt to the ground. He drove out of Los Angeles, past hotels and factories, until he reached the desert.

Haldeman had only visited Palm Springs once before, but he liked it and thought it was the ideal place to be while his plan was carried out. He turned on to Bob Hope Drive and drove towards Rancho Mirage, at the far end of Palm Springs. He thought about his plan yet again. The secret, he decided, was getting other people to do the dangerous work for you. All you needed was simple, loyal people who trusted you, like Larry Hyatt. And like José, the chef.

Hyatt had been employed by Haldeman as business manager for two years, and because of his unquestioning trust in his employer, he had produced completely false accounts for the last financial year. It had been simple enough to arrange.

According to the computer in Hyatt's office, the restaurant had enjoyed its best profits ever, with more customers in the last month than ever before. Hyatt rarely came to the restaurant. He knew little of the Mexican workers who were paid almost nothing, or of the nights when there was not a single customer. His accounts were based on false information and wage packets that did not exist. Even when the figures had been put into the computer, they were not safe from Haldeman, who had carefully altered them, just a little at a time. Poor old Hyatt never suspected a thing.

Why pretend the restaurant was making a profit? So that the insurance company would not suspect anything when they came to check the accounts of a recently burnt-down restaurant. They'd have suspicions about a place if business was bad. But a place as successful as this? Never!

▣ ▣ ▣

Haldeman parked in front of the Ranchero Motel. It was an old wooden building which needed painting. It had ten small rooms set around a courtyard, and a swimming pool that was rarely cleaned. But for Haldeman, there couldn't be a better place.

The man behind the desk wore a sweat-stained T-shirt and

had a day-old beard. Haldeman wrote his name in the guest book, making sure that his writing was clear and the date was correct. He knew the book would be checked. It was obvious that he was the only person staying at the Ranchero Motel. You had to be crazy to come to Palm Springs in August. It was a time when the relaxing warmth of the dry desert air turned to a fierce heat.

Haldeman put his bag in his room, then drove downtown and ate a large, expensive meal. He returned to the motel with some beer in one hand and a bucket of ice in the other.

The next day, his plan would begin. If he had any doubts about it, now was the time to stop the whole thing. But there was no other answer to his problems. He had to go ahead with it. He went into his room and opened a beer.

▦ ▦ ▦

Haldeman was woken at six-thirty by the sun on his face. He turned over on to his stomach. The sheets on the bed were a mess and he was sweating already.

In eight and a half hours, José would light the burners beneath the barbecue in the kitchen to prepare for the evening customers. At the same moment, Larry Hyatt had orders to call Haldeman from the manager's office above the restaurant. Haldeman had given Larry the phone number of the motel on Friday. He had also given him a small job to do at the restaurant on Saturday afternoon. This ensured that Larry would be in the building as the crime took place, and as the restaurant began to burn.

Haldeman climbed out of bed, smiling. Before he left on Friday, he had partly blocked the gas taps on the kitchen burners so that when they were turned off for the night, two of the taps would remain half open. All the pipes under the barbecue would then slowly fill with gas. There would be no leak to the outside air, only a large amount of gas in the system just waiting for José to come and light it at three o'clock this afternoon.

Hyatt, calling from the manager's office, would probably be far enough away from the explosion not to get hurt. Unlike José, who would be blown to pieces.

Of course, there was always the chance that José would decide to light the gas early today, but that didn't matter. Hyatt would have more reason to phone his boss quickly, and Haldeman would still have his alibi confirmed by the phone call. He got dressed and opened the door of his room. The heat from outside hit him like a solid wall. He looked at his watch. Seven thirty-five. It wasn't surprising that nobody came here in August.

He walked over to the pool and put a hand into the water. It felt hot to his hand. All around the sun beat down on to the trees and buildings, and the air was heavy and still.

Haldeman drove out to a nearby café for breakfast and afterwards took a walk around town before returning to his car. Shop windows were dark and their doors had signs which read: SEE YOU IN SEPTEMBER! The effort of walking around in this fierce heat was too much and he returned to the motel. When he arrived, he found the front office open and went in.

'Hi!' said old Ricky, the motel manager. His face still needed a shave. 'You sleep OK last night?'

'I guess so. Didn't expect it to be so hot this morning.' Haldeman sat down in a chair by the desk. 'What do you think the temperature is?'

'Oh, a hundred and ten, hundred and fifteen, about now,' said Ricky, looking out of the window. 'You just wait till after lunch though, if you want to feel some *real* heat. It'll be up in the hundred and twenties by then.'

'Why do you stay here in August?' asked Haldeman.

'I have to get this place ready for when we get busy again. I'm having a new roof put on, and new tar and tiles put down in the courtyards where the ground's cracked open with the heat. I have to almost rebuild this place every summer. We get storms, and floods, and heatwaves in August that kill half the old people. You want a beer?' He pushed an ice-cold can of beer along the desk.

A short time later, Haldeman returned to his room. While he was waiting for his call, he decided to sit and read outside under one of the faded orange sunshades surrounding the swimming pool. After only a few minutes, he was asleep.

The book fell to the ground and Haldeman woke up. He was suddenly thirsty. Beyond the blue pool stood rows of trees, and beyond those lay the desert, and then the mountains. Somewhere over toward the front office, hidden by trees, Mexican workmen called to each other as they carried in new orange tiles ready for repairing the courtyard.

He got up and walked back to his room. Inside it was cool and dark. A quarter to one. Two and a quarter hours before José reduced his restaurant to a car park, and Haldeman was provided with a solid, unbreakable alibi. He would have to make sure he was near a phone when Hyatt's call came through.

It was at this point that Haldeman noticed the lack of a telephone in the room.

▨ ▨ ▨

'No, sir, one thing we haven't got yet is room phones,' said Ricky, picking at his teeth with a piece of paper. He sat behind the reception desk with what was left of a plate of fried chicken in front of him. 'We don't get asked for them. People come here to get away from them.'

'Listen, I'm expecting a very important phone call in a couple of hours,' said Haldeman. 'I gave them the number here . . .'

'Where did you get that from?' asked Ricky.

'From the telephone book.'

'Oh, *that* number, that's the old number.'

'You mean I won't get the call?'

'Oh, it rings here still, but it's out the back on the old pay phone now. We changed the numbers last year.'

Haldeman sat back, relieved. 'Where can I find the phone booth?' he asked, trying to sound as casual as possible.

'Just go out behind the workmen to the back courtyard and it's straight across.'

'Thanks. I'll see you later.' Haldeman got up from the chair and went out into the sun.

At two thirty, he left his room with a beach towel and a glass filled with ice and whisky. He knew he probably shouldn't drink whisky before the call, but he needed it.

Round the back of the motel he found a large courtyard. Along one side a pair of faded sun-beds stood in the shadow of the wall. In the opposite far corner of the courtyard stood the phone booth, little more than a pay phone on a metal stick. Below it, a faded phone book hung on a chain.

The heat in the courtyard was amazing. Protected from the desert winds, it lay sheltered and silent at the back of the motel grounds. Haldeman lay down on one of the sun-beds.

After a few minutes, he fell into a half-sleep, and began to imagine the chef coming into the restaurant. He would be surprised to see Hyatt there, and the two men would talk together for a minute or two. José would then walk on to the kitchen, put on his chef's clothes, and wash his hands.

Meanwhile, Hyatt would move up to the manager's office and sit at the desk with his papers. Haldeman turned on to his side and drank the whisky before lying back on the sun-bed.

It was so hot here, hot enough to start a barbecue restaurant that worked on the natural heat of the sun . . . yes, maybe that was what he would do . . . maybe . . .

The phone was ringing.

Haldeman sat up on the sun-bed and looked at his watch. It was exactly three o'clock. He must have fallen asleep. Jumping up, he looked around for his shoes and shirt, then across at the ringing telephone on the far side of the courtyard. He wiped his sweating face. The ground between him and the telephone would be burning hot, but he would have to run across. He couldn't afford to miss the call; his alibi depended on it.

He ran towards the telephone booth, running as lightly as possible, but had only taken three steps before becoming aware of something wrong. The pain which had begun to cut into his bare feet was obviously caused by the sun-baked ground, but the ground did not feel solid under his feet. At the next step the bottom of his right foot felt as if it was on fire, and he screamed. In the distance, the telephone rang on. He looked down and saw the floor of the courtyard boiling in the heat, and this time he was forced to pull his left leg forward to keep moving. The sharp movement tore a piece of skin from the bottom of his left foot, and he fell forward on to one hand and a knee, crying with pain.

He could see the telephone, no more than eight feet away, ringing and ringing. All around him the surface of the courtyard was boiling. The Mexican workmen had only finished putting down the new tar yesterday. They had covered the surface with sand, then moved on to another part of the grounds. But because

The ground did not feel solid under his feet.

of the fierce heat, the tar had failed to harden. And today, the sun had brought the tar back to an almost liquid state.

Unable to support his body on his burning hand and knee, Haldeman fell screaming, face down onto the courtyard. Liquid knives of fire burned into his skin. He tried to turn and pull himself free, but every time he moved more skin tore loose . . .

▣ ▣ ▣

Larry Hyatt slowly put down the telephone. That was strange. Haldeman had particularly asked him to call at this time. As it happened, he needed to speak to the boss anyway, as there was a problem with the restaurant. An hour ago, José the chef had called to say he was sick, and so far they had been unable to find another chef. It looked as if they would not be able to open at all tonight. Oh well, he would try again in a few minutes.

▣ ▣ ▣

Haldeman was stuck by his bleeding, raw face in the hot tar. His chest, knees, and legs were also stuck, and the more he struggled, the more he stuck. His screams became higher and higher as the hot black liquid finally touched his right eye and boiled it white.

When the telephone rang again, he was still alive, though not conscious. Blood and tar had dried across his torn back, and most of the skin from his head and body lay stuck in the tar.

Altogether Hyatt rang four times, and for the first three Haldeman was still alive. But then the sun pushed up the temperature a further few burning degrees.

▣ ▣ ▣

The red thing that had been Haldeman moved for the last time as the sound of the telephone faded in its ears, and the chances of healing its torn body in the coolness of the motel's reception office disappeared in the cruel, unforgiving heat.

36

The Voice in the Night

William Hope Hodgson

It was a dark, starless night. We were in the Northern Pacific ocean, on a calm sea. There was no wind at all, and our little ship was not moving. Our exact position I do not know. For a week, the sun had been hidden by a thin mist which had seemed to float above us, about the height of our masts, sometimes descending to cover the surrounding sea like a blanket.

As there was no wind, there was little to do, and I was the only man on deck. The crew, consisting of two men and a boy, were sleeping in their cabin, while Will – my friend, and the captain of our boat – was asleep in the other cabin.

Suddenly, from out of the darkness, came a cry:

'Schooner, ahoy!'

It was so unexpected that I did not answer immediately. It came again – a voice strangely low and inhuman, calling from somewhere on the dark sea to our left.

'Schooner, ahoy!'

'Hello!' I cried. 'What – What are you? What do you want?'

'You need not be afraid,' answered the strange voice, having probably noticed some uncertainty in my words. 'I am only an old . . . man.'

The pause sounded odd, but it was only afterwards that I considered its importance.

'Why don't you come nearer then?' I asked, annoyed that he had thought I was afraid.

'I – I can't. It wouldn't be safe. I—' He stopped, and then there was silence.

'What do you mean?' I asked. 'Where are you?'

I listened for a moment, but there was no answer. A sudden suspicion I could not explain came over me, and I quickly got a lighted lamp and knocked on the deck with my foot to wake up Will. Then I was at the side of the boat, throwing the yellow stream of light into the silent darkness.

I heard a slight, low cry and then the sound of a splash, as if someone had dipped oars into the water. Yet I cannot be certain I saw anything, except that with the first flash of light, there had been something on the water, where now there was nothing.

'Hello there!' I called. 'What game is this?'

But there were only the sounds of a boat being rowed away into the night.

Then I heard Will's voice. 'What's wrong, George?' he asked, coming across the deck.

I told him about the strange thing that had happened. He asked several questions, then, after a moment's silence, raised his hands to his lips and shouted:

'Boat, ahoy!'

From a long distance away came a faint reply, and my companion repeated his call. After a short silence, we heard the sound of oars, and a voice said: 'Put away that light.'

'Never!' I replied, but Will told me to do as the voice asked, so I did.

'Come nearer!' shouted Will. 'There's nothing to be frightened of here!'

'Will you promise not to show the light?' said the voice.

'Why are you so afraid of the light?' I shouted.

'Because—' began the voice, then stopped.

Will put his hand on my shoulder. 'Be quiet for a minute, George,' he said. 'Let me talk to him.'

He looked out into the darkness.

'Listen, friend,' he said. 'This is a strange thing to happen, you appearing out of the darkness in the middle of the Pacific. How can we know you're not dangerous? You say you're alone, but how can we be sure unless we see you? Why are you objecting to the light, anyway?'

As Will finished speaking, I heard the noise of the oars again, and then the voice came; but now from a greater distance, and sounding sad and without hope.

'I am sorry – sorry! I would not have troubled you, only I am hungry, and – so is she.' The voice died away, leaving only the sound of the oars again.

'Stop!' shouted Will. 'Come back! We'll keep the light hidden, if you don't like it.' He turned to me. 'This is all very strange, but I don't think there's anything to be afraid of, do you?'

'No,' I replied. 'I think the poor man's been wrecked around here, and gone crazy.'

The sound of the oars came nearer.

'Put the lamp away,' Will said, then went to the side of the boat and listened. I hid the lamp then stood beside him. The dipping of the oars stopped about ten metres away from us.

'Will you come nearer now?' asked Will. 'We have hidden the lamp.'

'I – I cannot,' replied the voice. 'I do not dare to come nearer. I do not dare even to pay you for the – the food.'

'That's all right,' said Will, and hesitated. 'You're welcome to as much food as you can take.'

'You are very good,' said the voice. 'May God, who understands everything, reward you—' It stopped suddenly.

'The – the lady?' said Will. 'Is she—?'

'I have left her behind on the island,' said the voice.

'What island?' I asked.

'I do not know its name,' answered the voice. 'I wish to God—!' it began, then stopped quickly.

'Can we send a boat for her?' asked Will.

'No!' shouted the voice. 'My God! No!' There was a moment's pause, then the voice went on, 'It was because we needed food that I came, because of her terrible hunger.'

'Just wait, and I will bring you something at once,' said Will. And in a couple of minutes he was back, his arms full of food. 'Can you come nearer for it?' he asked.

'No – *I do not dare*,' replied the voice. And I realized, suddenly, that the poor old creature out there in the darkness was *suffering* because of his need for the things Will held in his arms; and yet, because of some terrible fear he could not express, was too afraid to come nearer our little schooner and receive them. And in the same moment I knew that he was not mad, but sanely facing some impossible horror.

Full of sympathy now, I said, 'Get a box, Will. We must float the stuff to him in it.'

This we did – pushing the box out into the darkness. A slight cry came from the creature out there, and we knew that he had it. A little later, he called out goodbye and warm thanks. Then we heard the dipping of oars in the darkness.

'I think he'll come back,' I said to Will. 'He must have badly needed that food.'

'He and the lady,' said Will.

For a moment he was silent, then he continued: 'It's the strangest thing that ever happened to me at sea.'

'Yes,' I said. 'And me.'

And so the time went past – an hour, and another, and still Will stayed with me, all desire to sleep gone after the strange adventure.

After nearly three hours, we heard the sound of oars again on the silent ocean.

'Listen!' said Will, excitement in his voice.

'He's coming,' I said.

The dipping oars came nearer, then stopped a little distance away. The voice came through the darkness again.

'Schooner, ahoy!'

'Is that you?' asked Will.

'Yes,' replied the voice. 'I left you suddenly, but – but there was great need.'

'The lady?' questioned Will.

'The – lady is grateful now on earth. She will be more grateful soon in – in heaven. She and I have spoken together. We had decided to leave this life without telling anyone about the terror which has come into our lives. Now she agrees with me that it is God's wish that we should tell you all that we have suffered since – since—'

'Yes?' said Will, softly.

'Since the sinking of our ship, the *Albatross*.'

'The *Albatross* left Australia to sail to San Francisco six months ago!' I said. 'And hasn't been seen or heard of since.'

'Yes,' answered the voice. 'We were caught in a terrible storm and the *Albatross*'s masts were broken. When the next day came, it was found that the ship was leaking badly, and when the sea was calm enough, the sailors took the small boats, leaving the lady – the lady I love – and myself on the wreck.

'We were in our cabin, getting a few of our things together, when they went, cruelly leaving us behind. When we came up on to the deck, they were far away. Yet we did not despair. We got to work and made a small raft. Upon this we put some food and water. The ship was now very low in the water, so we got on to the raft and pushed it off into the sea.

'We floated away and, after three hours, all we could see of the ship was its broken masts. Then, during the evening and through the night, it became misty. It remained that way for four days, and we floated through this strange mist until, on the evening of the fourth day, we could hear waves breaking against a shore in the distance.

'When morning came, we saw the shape of a large ship through the mist. It was close by, and we immediately thanked God because we thought here was an end to our dangers. We had much to learn.

'The raft got near to the ship and we shouted, but there was no answer. Soon after, the raft touched against the side of the ship and, seeing a rope hanging down, I seized it and began to climb. It was difficult because of a grey fungus which had wrapped itself around the rope and which was on the side of the ship.

'I reached the top and climbed on to the deck. Here I saw that the decks were covered in more of the grey fungus, some of it in shapes about two metres high. But at the time I was more interested in finding people on the ship. I shouted but nobody answered. Next I looked into some of the cabins, but there was a damp, sour smell in all of them and I knew immediately that there was nothing alive in there.

'I went back to the side where I had climbed up. My sweet love was still sitting quietly on the raft. She saw me and called up, asking if anyone was on the ship. I replied that the ship seemed to have been deserted for some time. Then I told her to wait while I looked for some sort of ladder for her to climb up, then we could search the ship together. A little later, on the opposite side of the deck, I found a rope ladder. I carried it across, and a minute afterwards, she was beside me.

'Together we explored the cabins, but there was no sign of life. Here and there we found some of that strange fungus. But this, we told ourselves, could be cleaned away.

'We were soon certain that there was nobody on the ship except the two of us and we began to make ourselves comfortable. Together we cleaned two of the cabins, then I searched the ship for anything we could eat. I soon found some food and fresh water, and thanked God for this.

'For several days we stayed on the ship without attempting to get to the shore. We started cleaning away pieces of fungus from the floors and walls of the cabins, but they returned to their original size within twenty-four hours, which depressed us and also made us feel uneasy. And by the end of the week, the fungus had spread into other places, as though by touching it we had somehow encouraged it to travel elsewhere.

'On the seventh morning, my dear love woke to find some of it on her pillow, close to her face. She dressed quickly and came to fetch me.

'"Come and look at this, John," she said. And after I saw the fungus on her pillow, we agreed to leave the ship and try to get to the shore and make ourselves comfortable there.

'We hurried to gather together our few things, and even

among these I found that the fungus had been at work. One of her dresses had a little piece of it growing near one edge. I threw the dress into the sea without saying anything to her.

'The raft was still in the water below, but I lowered a small boat that hung on the side of the ship, and in this we rowed across to the shore. But as we got near to it, I saw that the fungus was growing wildly there. In places it rose in horrible, fantastic shapes, which seemed almost to move like something alive when the wind blew across them. Here and there it took the shape of huge fingers, and in other places it just spread out flat and smooth and dangerous.

'At first there did not seem to be a part of the shore which was not hidden beneath the fungus. But after moving along the coast a little distance, we found a smooth white piece of what appeared to be fine sand, and there we landed. It was not sand. What it was I do not know. But I know now that the fungus will not grow on it. Everywhere else, except where the sand-like earth wanders like strange paths through the fungus, there is nothing but that horrible greyness.

'It is difficult to make you understand how happy we were to find one place free from the fungus, and here we put down our things. Then we went back to the ship for anything it seemed we might need. This included one of the ship's sails from which I made two small tents. In these we lived and kept our food, and for about four weeks everything went well.

'It was on the thumb of her right hand that the fungus first appeared. It was only a small circle but – my God! Fear filled my heart when she showed it to me. We cleaned it off, washing it with soap and water, but by the following day the thing had returned. Without speaking, we started to remove it again.

Suddenly, she said: "What's that on the side of your face, dear? Under the hair by your ear." I put a hand up to feel the place, and then I knew. "Let's get your thumb clean first," I said.

'I finished washing her thumb, and then she washed my face. After that we sat together and talked of many things, as sudden, very terrible thoughts had come into our lives. We were, all at once, afraid of something worse than death. We spoke of loading the boat with food and water and rowing out to sea, but we decided to stay. We would wait. God would decide what was to happen to us.

'A month, two months, three months passed and the fungus grew bigger, and more grew on our faces and bodies. From time to time we went back to the ship to get more food. We had now stopped thinking about leaving the island. How could we go among healthy humans? It was not possible. Knowing this, we were careful with our food and water, since we might continue to live for many years yet. But then I discovered that there was very little left of the ship's store of hard bread. So I began fishing in the sea. Sometimes I caught a fish but it was little help in keeping us from the hunger which threatened. It seemed to me that we were more likely to die from hunger than from the fungus that was growing on our bodies.

'Then, one morning when the ship's bread was almost gone, I saw my sweet love eating something in her tent. When she saw me, she quickly threw away whatever it was. Suddenly suspicious, I walked across and picked it up. It was a piece of the grey fungus. I carried it across to her in my hand, and she turned deadly pale, then red.

'I was frightened. "My dear! My dear!" I said, and could say no more. She began to cry bitterly. When at last she was calm

45

'We were, all at once, afraid of something worse than death.'

again, she admitted that she had tried eating it the day before and
– and liked it. I got her to promise not to touch it again, however
great our hunger.

'Later that day I walked along one of the paths through the
fungus. I went much farther than usual, and suddenly I heard a
strange, rough sound on my left. Turning quickly, I saw
something move among an extraordinary shape of fungus, close
to my elbow. As I stared, the thought came to me that the thing
looked like the bent figure of a human creature. Even as this
thought flashed into my brain, there was a slight, sickening noise
of tearing, and I saw that one of the branch-like arms was
separating itself from the surrounding grey fungus, and coming
towards me. The head of the thing, a shapeless grey ball, nodded
at me. I stood stupidly, and the horrible arm brushed across my
face. I screamed and moved away. There was a sweet taste on
my lips where the thing had touched me. I licked them, and was
immediately filled with a desire that was not human. I seized
some of the fungus and pushed it into my mouth. More – and
more! I could not stop myself!

'Suddenly, I remembered my discovery that morning, my
sweet love's face, her shame – and I threw the fungus in my hand
on to the ground. Then, feeling a terrible guilt, I walked back to
our little camp.

'I think she knew as soon as she saw me. Her quiet sympathy
made it easier for me, and I told her of my sudden weakness. I
did not mention the thing which had happened just before – the
'arm' that had brushed my face. I wanted to save her from
unnecessary terror.

'But, for myself, this new knowledge filled me with unending
terror. I had no doubt that I had seen, in that monstrous grey

shape, the end of one of those men who had come to the island in the ship. And in that dreadful ending I had seen our own.

'After that, we kept away from the horrible food, although the desire for it had entered our blood. But day after day the fungus took hold of our poor bodies. There was nothing we could do to stop it. And so we, who had been human, became – well, it does not matter now. Every day the fight against the hunger for the fungus is more dreadful. A week ago we ate the last of the ship's bread, and since then I have caught three fish. I was out fishing tonight when your schooner came out of the mist. I called to you, and – well, you know the rest.'

There was the dip of an oar, and then another. Then the voice came again, and for the last time, through the mist.

'God be with you! Goodbye!'

'Goodbye!' we shouted together, our hearts full of many emotions.

I looked around, and became aware that daylight had crept up on us. A thin line of sunlight cut through the mist to shine down on the boat as it moved away. I saw something nodding between the oars – a great, grey, nodding shape. The oars and the boat were also grey. Then the boat moved out of the light, and the – the *thing* went nodding into the mist.

The Whispering Gallery

William F. Temple

'**N**ow, if you will just come this way. . .'
The voice was smooth and silky. It suggested that wonders
existed which would make all you had seen so far become thin
and flat and forgotten. Amazing things lay just around the corner
and the voice knew the way.

But Frederic was five years old and therefore he knew what
voices really said and it wasn't always what the words seemed
to mean. This voice said, really, 'I hate you all, especially the boy,
and this is the way out and I shall be glad to see the last of you.'

The voice did not intend, after all, to lead the way up the secret
stairs to the golden ball.

The guide was a tall thin man, with a yellow hollowed face and
eye-holes so deep and shadowed you could not be sure whether
there were eyes in them or not. Not unless you looked hard into
them, and so far Frederic had not found the courage to do that.

Now and then he glanced up at the guide's face but each time
he was frightened away by the sight of the strangely small nose
and the almost lipless mouth with the big white teeth that seemed
to be fixed in a bitter grin.

Yesterday was the magic morning when Jim was driving him
around London in the open-top car. Just him and Jim. They were
stopped in busy traffic in Fleet Street.

'Look!' said Frederic, pointing over the front of the car. 'That
must be the biggest building in the world!'

The driver looked up at the Cathedral.

'It looks big from here because it's standing on top of a hill – Ludgate Hill,' he said. 'But it's not as big as the Empire State Building in New York, and you've been up that.'

Frederic tipped his head back as far as it would go. The great dome was like an enormous bubble, and on top stood a high tower with a golden gallery around the bottom. And at the top of this tower was a golden ball with a golden cross on it. All the golden things shone in the sunlight but the ball shone brightest of all.

'Don't be stupid, Jim,' said Frederic. 'It's much higher than the Empire State Building. It's the biggest thing I've ever seen. And look at that lovely golden ball! I wish I had it to play with. I wonder if it – comes off?'

'Would you like me to climb up there and fetch it for you?' asked Jim with a smile.

'Would you?' said Frederic, eagerly. '*Would* you?'

Jim laughed. There was a time when he would have sighed and murmured under his breath, 'These rich people are all alike. Get me this, get me that, they say. Look, the moon shines pretty – get me that!'

But he had been driving for them for a long time now and he knew that they were always wanting something. Not only to have something but to go somewhere, see something new, have someone praise them, do things for them. They were always hoping to discover something that shone bright and new to fascinate them. Like the golden ball on the top of St Paul's Cathedral on a sunny day when you were five years old.

'Jim! You're not listening. Get me the ball, Jim.'

'It's much, much bigger than you think, Freddy. When you're

small, you don't realize the size things are. Six grown-up men could get inside that ball.'

'It's no bigger than an apple!' said Frederic. 'Perhaps it *is* an apple – a golden apple. I've always wanted a golden apple. I wonder if it is, Jim? Do you think it is?'

Jim Bates opened his mouth, then closed it again. He had often done that in the service of the Staggs. Mrs Stagg frequently found the truth unpleasant. Her son also believed only what he wanted to believe.

'I don't know, Freddy. We must go back to the hotel now,' said Jim, quickly but firmly. 'Your mother said that you were to be back at one o'clock for lunch.'

'Oh,' said Frederic, disappointed.

The car turned left at Ludgate Circus, then went through the side streets to Holborn and back to the hotel at Marble Arch. Frederic kept looking back, but he could not see St Paul's again because of the shops and office buildings. He couldn't understand how such little buildings could hide it.

◧ ◧ ◧

'But I can't, Frederic – not this afternoon,' said Mrs Stagg. 'We're having tea with Lady Cornford.'

'Can we go tomorrow then, Mom?'

'No, we're going home tomorrow.'

The corners of Frederic's mouth turned down. There were tears in his eyes.

'Oh, dear!' said Mrs Stagg, anxious to prevent her son's noisy screams. 'Well, look, I could just spare half an hour – no more.'

Frederic smiled. 'Thanks, Mom.' Half an hour was a long time. Easily long enough to reach the golden apple.

It was a long time but Skeleton-face, as Frederic silently named

51

the guide, wasted it. When he had taken the little group around the Cathedral, Frederic hoped that now they would go up to the golden ball.

But the quiet, cold voice said, 'Now, if you will just come this way . . .'

And it led them down the stairs into the underground rooms where some of England's most famous people were buried. This cold, shadowy place seemed like the natural home of the voice. It seemed to Frederic that the voice wanted none of them to leave, it wanted them all to stay here. It would talk smoothly and quietly until it sent them to sleep and then, somehow, it would get them to lie <u>stiff</u> and dead with the others under the hard stone floor.

'I want to go upstairs!' Frederic said.

That was when the voice began to hate him.

'Now, if you will just come this way . . .'

They went upstairs, past a notice saying *To the Golden Gallery and Ball* and up some more stairs, up and up and up.

As they climbed behind the guide, Frederic became excited. Maybe this guide wouldn't *give* him the ball (which, of course, was really an apple) but if Mom saw how much he wanted it she would buy it for him. It didn't matter how much it cost – Mom was the richest lady in the world. She could buy him the whole Cathedral if she wanted to. But he only wanted the apple.

The richest lady in the world was breathing heavily as she climbed. 'Oh dear! I didn't know it was going to take as long as this,' she said.

They got to the top of the stairs and Frederic followed the guide through the only doorway there.

'*Ooh!*' they all said when they found they were standing on a narrow ledge which went right round the inside of the great dome. Only an iron rail stood between them and the ground, far, far below, where tiny people the size of insects moved around.

Frederic looked up and saw that, although he was very high up, the golden apple was at least as high again above him. There must be more stairs somewhere that led up through the dome. Perhaps some secret stairs.

He hesitated and tried to go back but the heavy grown-ups around him pushed him forward. And then they stopped because the guide had stopped.

Skeleton-face said, 'This is the famous Whispering Gallery. If you would please move around to the opposite side and stand listening against that wall . . .'

'I don't want—' began Frederic. But Mrs Stagg grabbed his hand and said in a low, annoyed whisper, 'Oh, come *on*!'

The group moved slowly round, with the fearful drop on its right-hand side. Some glanced down, but others dared not look. All were silent. Frederic wanted to run, but the Cathedral was a place where you neither ran nor shouted.

At last they reached the side of the Gallery opposite the doorway where the guide had remained standing, made tiny by the distance. They arranged themselves in a line, kneeling with one knee on the seat, putting one ear close to the wall.

Frederic did not put his ear very close. He did not wish to hear that voice again. But he did hear it, loud and clear, as if the guide were standing beside him – yet he could see him, a long way away with all the width of the dome between them.

'I am speaking only in a whisper, yet you hear me clearly. The pictures you can see on the inside of the dome were painted by Sir James Thornhill. They show events in the life of St Paul . . .'

Frederic put his mouth close to the wall. 'We don't want to stay here,' he said. 'We want to go up to the golden apple.'

'Frederic!' said his mother, shocked and alarmed. Her voice sounded amazingly loud under the great hollow dome.

The guide's voice had stopped. There was a moment's awful silence, during which Mrs Stagg's face became redder and redder.

Then – 'Now, if you will just come this way . . .'

The voice was smooth and silky. It suggested that wonders existed which would make all you had seen so far become thin and flat and forgotten.

But Frederic was five years old and therefore he knew that the voice really said, 'I hate you all, especially the boy, and this is the way out and I shall be glad to see the last of you.'

The voice did not intend, after all, to lead the way up the secret stairs to the golden ball.

The group moved round the great half-circle back to the door and to Skeleton-face. Frederic would not look up. He knew that deep in those dark eye-holes hatred burned like a flame and if the other people hadn't been there . . . He was glad now that he was in the middle of a group of grown-ups who could protect him.

Staying close he watched his feet and his mother's feet descending the stairs. And soon they were crossing the black-and-white floor, then the dirty black steps outside the Cathedral.

He saw the car and Jim's smiling face, and the fear inside him slowly disappeared.

'Get in, Frederic, don't just stand there,' said his mother, pushing him. 'Go as fast as you dare, Bates. We're ten minutes late now. What *will* Lady Cornford think of us?'

Frederic's behaviour was not at its best at Lady Cornford's. He was silent and, when forced to speak, rude – very rude.

When they got back to the hotel, Mrs Stagg punished him by sending him straight to bed. But he did not feel any guilt, only an aching regret that tomorrow they would be leaving London and leaving the golden apple behind. Someone else would come along and take the golden apple away while he was on the silly ship or back at the silly school in Boston.

He got out of bed and went to the window. He watched the buses moving in and out of Park Lane, and the people in Hyde Park. It was summer and there was still an hour or two before it would be dark.

Suddenly it seemed as if someone else had taken control of his body and was making it do things he hadn't yet decided to do. He found himself putting on his clothes and opening the door quietly. Then he was at the open window at the back of the building, climbing through it and descending the iron steps of the fire-escape.

It was a straight road back to St Paul's, but it was a very long road and his feet were tired as he climbed the dirty steps in the pale, rose-coloured light coming up the hill from the sinking sun.

He entered through the big doors and heard the sound of singing. At the other end of the building he saw the two lines of singers, and the people watching them.

No one noticed him move quickly between the chairs and up the stairs which led to the Whispering Gallery. All the guides would have left, including Skeleton-face. All he had to do was find a place to hide for a little while until everyone went home.

Up the stairs he had noticed a corner where he could hide. He hoped he could reach it soon because his legs were aching and he was very tired . . .

When he woke up, his legs and shoulders hurt after being curled up in that tight little corner. Rubbing them, he went exploring in the dark. How could he find the secret stairs to the apple? He wished he had remembered to bring a torch, but he hadn't intended to fall asleep and stay here until after it was dark.

He was not afraid because the ball shining in the sunlight still shone in his memory, and he felt that it was still shining somewhere above him. When he reached it and picked it (for it was just an apple really), it would continue to shine and light his way back down the stairs and along the streets to the hotel.

He bumped into and half-fell along the wall, then fell through a doorway. As he lay there, his foot discovered the top of some stairs.

And then, quite clearly, he heard the slow steady sound of feet coming up those dark stairs.

He must not be discovered! He got up quickly and went on through the doorway. He was in the Whispering Gallery now, lit by the pale yellow light of the moon.

He hesitated. There was only one door, which was both the entrance to and exit from the Gallery. The footsteps were louder now and began to echo. He ran from them, trying to make no noise, and keeping close to the seat along the curving wall.

Yet he was still not really frightened – only excited.

At a place exactly opposite the door, the place where they had all stood listening that afternoon, he sat on a seat, curled against the wall, trying to make himself small so that he could not be seen. He held his breath, afraid that the wall would catch the small sound and send it echoing noisily round the dome.

A cloud moved away from the moon, and the dark doorway on the far side of the Gallery became visible. Below, in the

Cathedral, he saw now that there were a few little circles of electric light in the darkness.

But now he watched the doorway opposite – and waited.

Soon a thin black shadow separated itself from the doorway. Then the cloud thickened under the moon and the shadow became part of the blackness.

He sat holding the edge of the seat, trembling a little but not really afraid. Then his heart jumped into his throat as the voice spoke right beside him. A voice coldly polite but full of evil. '*Now, if you will just come this way . . .*'

His trembling became a violent shaking and a pain grabbed his stomach. His breath came in loud rapid gasps and, for what seemed a long time, he sat staring with terror through the rail at the lights below – as far away as stars – afraid to look up at Skeleton-face standing over him. Afraid to look at the deep, shadowed eye-holes and the white fixed smile. Shrinking from the imagined touch of a thin hand.

But no hand touched him.

Then the moon broke free of the cloud, throwing silvery light around him, and he saw that the shadow remained small and distant by the door. He began to hope it was not a man at all but the shadow of some ordinary thing he had not noticed before. Yet it had seemed to move . . .

He watched it, relaxing slowly as the thin shadow remained stiff and unmoving.

But he had not imagined the voice, which had been real enough. Perhaps everything you said in the Whispering Gallery went echoing round the Gallery for ever and ever because there was no way for it to get out. Like a fly caught in an upside-down bowl.

All he had heard was an echo of the words Skeleton-face had kept using in the afternoon.

Then he jumped again, as the same cold voice said right beside him, '*If you will just come this way . . .*'

He began sweating, but he told himself that it was all right. The shadow hadn't moved, it was only that old echo again.

He noticed it had dropped a word this time. How could the sound of the word '*Now*' have escaped? But of course! It would have slipped out through the doorway as the echo went past. That was how echoes died, losing a piece every time they went slowly round. That had to be true, otherwise everything everybody ever said would go round and round for ever, like a great crowd shouting all the time.

Well, he couldn't just sit there. He had to find the stairs that went up to the golden apple. His mother might have already discovered that he wasn't in the hotel, and would guess where he had gone and come after him.

He stood up slowly, not taking his eyes off the shadow by the door. It remained still. And then the clouds covered the moon and the silvery light disappeared, and it was darker than ever.

He could not go around the Gallery in the darkness. But if there was no light, there could be no shadow. However, his fear was too strong, and he stood there holding the rail and looking down at the little lights below. Suddenly he wished he was down there in the safe steady light that did not go out and leave you trapped on a high shelf and at the mercy of unseen shadows.

But if he was down there he would be further away from the shining golden apple. To obtain that prize he had to be brave.

His fingers became tight on the rail as the voice from the dark said, '*You will just come this way . . .*'

This time it sounded less like a request and more like an order. '*You* will *just come this way . . .*'

Frederic thought, It's all right really. If I stay here long enough the echo will have no more words left, it will die and perhaps the shadow will go with it.

He was glad when the bright moonlight suddenly flooded the dome again. Or he was until—

He screamed as he saw that the shadow had moved nearly halfway around the Gallery in the darkness and was still moving steadily towards him.

He turned and ran in the opposite direction. But the shadow had turned back and was moving quickly the other way to get to him before he could reach the door. And it was moving faster than he could run.

He turned round, gasping with terror, thin little screams coming from his mouth as he ran. For now he knew that the shadow was the shadow of Death. And Death wanted to take him and put him with the other dead people under the cold floor of the Cathedral.

He was opposite the door again, and the shadow was back at the doorway. He fell on to the seat, gasping for breath.

Then the voice came again, quietly this time, and softly persuasive, '*Just come this way . . .*'

It was a trap! He would not go. But there was still hope because the voice had lost two of its words this time.

The great dome was now full of moonlight and the human figures in the pictures were like a silent audience, looking down at him. St Paul seemed to be watching him. He stood up there, one hand pointing towards the top of the dome and the golden apple. 'That's the way you want to go, Frederic,' his face said.

'I know, I know,' whispered the boy. 'But how do I get up there?'

And the voice of Death spoke again, calling, *'Come this way . . .'*

'No!' cried Frederic, jumping up and moving away from the seat. The shadow moved in the same direction, coming around to meet him. He ran back and the shadow stopped, as if it were watching him and trying to guess what he intended to do, then it moved back to the doorway.

And so Frederic stopped again, knowing that he could never reach the door safely because the shadow could always get there first. Was there to be no end to this horrible game?

Yes, he thought desperately, *there must be an end when the echo dies. And that must be soon now.*

He put his hot forehead against the cool iron rail. There were, he noticed, pictures of angels just under the Gallery. Angels flying confidently.

He thought, *If only I had wings! I could escape Death and I could fly up there and pick the golden apple.*

His forehead burned and his head ached. The angels seemed to advance and move away again as if they were flying over the back wall. He watched them for some time, and they seemed to smile and indicate that it was quite easy to fly. Anyone could do it. *He* could do it if only he tried.

Then suddenly he remembered the shadow and looked at the opposite side of the Gallery. And it was gone!

But he saw a movement to his right, and there was a shadow, much taller, well past the halfway mark on its way to him. Even if Frederic ran his fastest, the shadow could catch him easily before he could reach the door.

It was Skeleton-face. He could see the dark eye-holes and the white teeth as the tall thin figure approached.

Frederic climbed up on to the rail, balancing there. He looked up. Somewhere beyond the dome was the shining prize he would never now reach.

But St Paul still pointed up and seemed to say, 'Have faith! Have faith!'

And the angels seemed to be calling to him: 'Have faith, Frederic, and you can fly like us. Have faith and you can fly up to the apple.'

Skeleton-face was almost beside Frederic now, his mouth open to speak.

'*This way . . .*'

'You can fly. You can fly. Have faith,' called the angels.

'I have faith. I'm coming,' said Frederic with a new strength. He began to step forward, quite steadily and calmly.

'*Frederic!*' It was his mother's voice, loud with alarm.

A warm relief flooded over him. Mom had found him, had got here just in time. She would save him. She would pay Skeleton-face to go away. She could pay anything, she was so rich.

He looked eagerly around but he couldn't see her. There was only Skeleton-face reaching for him.

Suddenly he realized that the cry was only the echo of his mother's exclamation that afternoon. It must have been slowly moving in circles, round the Gallery, ever since.

He was sick with disappointment.

And then a bony hand reached for his ankle . . . and he jumped out into space.

It wasn't a jump of faith. It was a jump to avoid death.

In confusion and misery he fell past the angels, fell into

darkness. The electric lights grew bigger as he fell and they shone on something that lay below them.

A golden disc . . .

He was going straight towards it. Could it be that somehow he was succeeding after all? That he was to reach—?

The golden disc flashed up hugely now, blinding him.

▣ ▣ ▣

The night verger had glanced up to see what looked like a tiny figure balancing on the rail of the Whispering Gallery. And as he watched, it jumped out into space.

'*My God!*' he said, and rushed forward.

A thin shout came from above. '*Way . . .!*'

He watched the figure fall until it hit the large round brass plate in the floor. It was immediately above the place where Nelson was buried, and immediately under the ball and cross 365 feet above. The verger hid his eyes.

When he looked again, small rivers of blood were spreading from the broken little shape that lay on the brass plate.

It was a small boy, a child. Dead, of course.

He went to find the other night verger and brought him to see it. But now the brass plate shone clean and bright – and clear. There was no body. There was no blood.

The second verger put his arm round the other, who had suddenly begun to shake. He led him to a chair.

'Don't worry, Alex,' he said. 'It's all right. It once happened to me.'

Alex looked at him in slow surprise, his hands shaking like those of a very old man.

'Nor are we the only ones,' said the second verger. 'It happens – every now and then.'

'When did it first – *really* – happen?'

'More than twenty years ago. It was a boy named Stagg – an American boy. He somehow found his way here and got up there. He had been here in the afternoon and for some reason wanted very much to return. He was due to go home the next

And then a bony hand reached for his ankle . . .

day, so his mother guessed he might have come here. But she got here just too late – he was already on the rail, just as you and I saw him. She shouted his name, but he fell.'

Alex looked up at the dome. 'He jumped,' he said in a low voice. 'But he saw me. He must have thought he was going to hit me. He shouted "*Way!*"'

'*Someone* shouted "Way!" I heard it too when it happened to me. But it didn't sound like a boy's voice. He was only five.'

'Then who was it?'

The second verger looked around uneasily. 'There have been many temples in this place, going back centuries,' he said. 'Before this there were at least three other Christian churches, and long before that the Romans had a temple here – for very different gods . . .' His voice faded away, then he looked at Alex. 'What terrifies me is this: does that poor child have to suffer his dreadful experience over and over again, every time it happens? Is he caught in some cruel circle of time and unable to escape?'

'I don't think so,' said Alex. 'What's past is past. By some trick of time, we have seen that past – like looking at an old film where the characters are only shadows.'

They sat side by side under the great dome in a little pool of light, each grateful that the other was there. All around them were black shadows, and under their feet were the bones of the dead. The great and the small. The famous and the forgotten. The human and the – possibly non-human.

'Now, if you will just come this way . . .'

The voice was smooth and silky. It suggested that wonders existed which would make all you had seen so far become thin and flat and forgotten. Amazing things lay just around the corner and the voice knew the way . . .

Ringing the Changes

s soon as they entered the town of Holihaven, walking from the railway station with their luggage, a church bell began to ring, its single deep note echoing through the darkness.

'What narrow streets!' said Phrynne.

'They follow the lines of the old city,' said Gerald. 'Holihaven was once one of the most important seaports in Britain.'

'Where *is* everybody?'

Although it was only six o'clock, the place seemed deserted.

'Do you think we're in the right street for the Bell Hotel?' said Gerald.

'Probably not,' she said. 'But there's no one to ask.'

The single deep notes of the bell were now coming more frequently.

'Why are they ringing that bell?' she asked. 'Is it a funeral?'

'Bit late for a funeral,' he said. 'I hope it isn't going to ring all night.'

'Look! We've passed it.'

They stopped and he looked back. She was right. They walked back and entered the hotel. A woman who seemed to be the landlady came forward to greet them.

'Mr and Mrs Banstead?' she said. 'I'm Hilda Pascoe. Don, my husband, isn't very well.'

Gerald felt full of doubts. He had chosen the hotel from a guide book and was already regretting it. It was partly Phrynne's fault for insisting that they go somewhere he did not know for their honeymoon.

'I'm sorry to hear that,' said Phrynne. 'What's the trouble?'

'It's always the same trouble with Don,' said Mrs Pascoe, then hesitated. 'It's his stomach,' she said.

Gerald interrupted, 'Could we see our room?'

'So sorry,' said Mrs Pascoe. 'Will you sign the hotel book first?' She passed the book to Gerald. He wrote his name and address, and noticed that the last visitors in the book had been several weeks ago. 'We're always quiet in October,' said Mrs Pascoe, watching him.

'Are we alone in the hotel?' asked Gerald.

'Except for Commandant Shotcroft. He's a resident.'

'What's that bell?' asked Gerald. Apart from anything else, the sound was much too near.

Mrs Pascoe looked away quickly. 'Practice,' she said.

'Do you mean there will be more of them later?'

She nodded. 'But let me take you to your room.'

Before they had reached the bedroom, the whole peal of bells had begun. 'Is this the quietest room you have?' asked Gerald. 'What about the other side of the house?'

'This *is* the other side of the house. Saint Guthlac's church is over there.' She pointed out through the bedroom door.

'Darling,' said Phrynne, her hand on Gerald's arm, 'they'll soon stop. They're only practising.'

Mrs Pascoe said nothing. Her expression indicated that if Gerald and Phrynne chose to leave, they were free to do so.

'What time's dinner?' Gerald asked her.

'Seven-thirty. You've time for a drink in the bar first.'

She went away.

'Actually, I *like* church bells,' said Phrynne. She stood by the window looking down into the street. 'There's still no one around.'

'I expect they're all in the bar,' said Gerald.

'I don't want a drink. I want to explore the town and look at the sea.'

Mrs Pascoe was not around when they went downstairs, nor were there sounds of anyone else in the hotel. Outside, the noise of the bells seemed to be immediately over their heads.

'Do you think the sea's down there?' shouted Phrynne. She pointed down the street, which seemed to end in nothing. 'Come on, let's run!'

There was nothing for him to do except run after her. Then she stopped and held her arms wide to catch him. The top of her head hardly came up to his chin.

'Isn't it beautiful?' she said.

'The sea?' There was no moon, and little could be seen beyond the end of the street.

'You can smell it,' she said.

'I certainly can't hear it.'

She turned her head away from him. 'The bells echo so much, it's as if there were two churches.'

'I'm sure there are more than that. There always are in old towns like this.'

'Yes,' cried Phrynne, delighted. 'It *is* another church.'

'Impossible,' said Gerald. 'Two churches wouldn't practise ringing on the same night.'

'I'm quite sure. I can hear one lot of bells with my left ear, and another lot with my right.'

They had still seen no one.

She held his hand. 'Let's go down on the beach and look for the sea.' They descended some steps on to a stony beach. 'We'll go straight on until we find it.'

Gerald was less keen to walk across the large, slippery stones in the dark.

'You're right, Phrynne, about the smell,' he said.

'An honest sea smell,' she said.

He thought it was more like the smell of something rotten. After what seemed a very long time, Phrynne spoke again.

'Gerald, where is it? What sort of seaport has no sea?'

She walked on, but Gerald stopped and looked back at the lights of the town. He was shocked to see how far they had come. He turned to look at Phrynne but could hardly see her.

Unexpectedly she gave a sharp cry.

'Phrynne!' he called.

She did not answer.

'Phrynne!'

Then she spoke more or less calmly. 'It's all right. Sorry, darling. I stood on something.'

He struggled up to her. 'The smell's worse than ever.'

'I think it's coming from what I stepped on. My foot went right in, and then there was the smell.'

'Let's go back. Yes?'

'Yes,' said Phrynne. 'But I'm disappointed not to see the sea.'

'The whole place is a disappointment,' he said. 'We'll go somewhere else.'

'I like the bells,' she replied carefully. 'And I don't want to go somewhere where you've been before for our honeymoon.'

Back at the hotel, they went to the Coffee Room and sat at a table under a lamp which was hardly bright enough to cut through the shadows. At first they thought they were alone, but then saw a man sitting by himself at an unlighted corner table. In the darkness he looked like a monkey.

'Why are you here?' he asked them.

Phrynne looked frightened, but Gerald replied quietly, 'We're on holiday. I suppose you are Commandant Shotcroft?'

'No need to suppose,' he said. He switched on the lamp nearest to him. He had finished his meal and Gerald realized that he must have switched off the light when he had heard them approaching. 'I'm going anyway.'

'Are we late?' asked Phrynne.

'No,' said the Commandant in a deep voice. 'I like to eat alone.' He stood up. 'So perhaps you'll excuse me.' Without waiting for an answer, he walked quickly out of the room. He had short white hair and a sad round face.

A second later his head appeared round the door again. 'Ring,' he said, and disappeared once more.

'Too many other people ringing,' said Gerald. 'But I don't see what else we can do.'

The Coffee Room bell made a noise like a fire alarm.

Mrs Pascoe appeared, unsteady on her feet. She seemed to have drunk a large amount of alcohol. They ordered their meal and Mrs Pascoe served it to them.

'Coffee is served in the next room,' she told them when they had finished.

They went into the next room. The noise of the bells came from all around. After two cups of coffee, Gerald suddenly said, 'Every church in town must be ringing its bells. They haven't stopped for two and a half hours!' He stood up. 'I think I'll get us both a drink from the bar.'

The bar was as empty as everywhere else in the hotel and the town. There was not even a person to serve him. Annoyed, he struck a brass bell which he saw hanging there, and Mrs Pascoe appeared at a door at the end of the bar.

He ordered a brandy for himself and a whisky for Phrynne. Mrs Pascoe's hands were shaking so much that she could not open the brandy bottle. Gerald did it for her, then she poured brandy into a glass. But when she reached for the whisky bottle, she knocked the brandy bottle on to the floor and smashed it.

A fat, red-faced man appeared at the door at the end of the bar. He held on to the doorway with each red hand, and began to shout at Mrs Pascoe. He was too drunk for his words to make any sense, and even across the bar his breath smelled strongly of whisky. Gerald assumed this was Don. He saw that Mrs Pascoe was about to start crying and something made him say, 'Sorry about the accident.'

Mrs Pascoe looked at him. Slow, desperate tears slipped down her cheeks. 'Mr Banstead, can I come and sit with you and your wife for a few minutes?'

'Yes, of course,' he said. It was not what he wanted, but he felt sorry for her.

They were in the other room when she remembered the whisky for Phrynne. 'It doesn't matter,' Gerald told her.

Phrynne had fallen asleep in the chair. Gerald thought that she looked very beautiful. Commandant Shotcroft was standing silently behind her, looking down at her.

'Will you join us?' Gerald asked him.

The Commandant did not turn his head and seemed unable to speak. Then in a low voice he said, 'For a moment only.'

The events in the bar had made Gerald forget about the bells.

Now, as they sat silently round the sleeping Phrynne, the tide of sound swept over him once more.

'You mustn't think that he's always like that,' Mrs Pascoe said, meaning her husband. 'We ought never to have come here. We were happy in South Norwood.'

'What made you leave?' asked Gerald.

'Don's stomach. The doctor said he needed sea air.'

'We went down on the beach before dinner,' said Gerald. 'We couldn't see the sea anywhere.'

'I never have time to look at the sea,' said Mrs Pascoe. She glanced uneasily at the Commandant, then stood up. 'Now I must get on with my work.'

When Mrs Pascoe had left, the Commandant spoke.

'He was a fine man once.'

'Pascoe?'

The Commandant nodded. 'They didn't leave South Norwood for the sea air. He got into trouble. He wasn't the sort of man to know how rotten people can be.'

'A pity,' said Gerald. 'Perhaps this isn't the best place for him.'

'It's the worst,' said the Commandant, a dark flame in his eyes. 'For him or anyone else.'

Phrynne moved in her sleep and both men remained silent until she was breathing steadily again. Against the silence within, the bells sounded louder than ever. It was as if the noise was tearing holes in the roof.

'It's certainly a very noisy place,' said Gerald, quietly.

'Why did you have to come tonight of all nights?'

'This doesn't happen often?'

'Once every year.'

'They should have told us,' said Gerald.

'They don't usually take visitors. When Pascoe was managing the place, they never did. This is Mrs Pascoe's doing.'

'I expect she thought they needed the business,' said Gerald.

'At heart women are creatures of darkness all the time.'

The Commandant's bitterness left Gerald without a reply. After a moment he said, 'My wife doesn't mind the bells.'

The Commandant stared at him. 'Take her away, man,' he said fiercely. 'Now. While there's still time. This instant.'

'They can't go on practising all night,' said Gerald.

'They're not practising!' the Commandant said coldly. 'They're ringing to wake the dead.'

Gerald's face went very pale and he turned to look at Phrynne. His voice dropped to a whisper. 'What happens?'

The Commandant, too, was nearly whispering. 'No one knows how long they have to go on ringing. It varies from year to year, but you should be all right until midnight. In the end, the dead awake. First one or two, then all of them. Tonight even the sea moves back. You've seen that yourself. In a place like this there are always several drowned each year. This year there have been more than several. But most of them come not from the water but from the earth.'

'Where do they go?'

'I've never followed them to see. I'm not mad.'

There was a long pause.

'So you advise me to go,' said Gerald. 'But I have no car.'

'Then walk,' said the Commandant. 'She's young and strong. Twenty years younger than you and therefore twenty years more important.'

'Yes,' said Gerald. 'I agree . . . What will you do?'

'I've lived here for some time now. I know what to do.'

Suddenly Phrynne sat up. 'Hello,' she said, not completely awake. 'What fun! The bells are still ringing.'

The Commandant stood up. 'You've still got time,' he told Gerald. Then he nodded to Phrynne, and left the room.

'What have you still got time for?' asked Phrynne, stretching.

'Nothing important,' said Gerald.

'Sorry I'm so sleepy. Shall we go for another walk? That would wake me up. And perhaps the sea has come in.'

Gerald found it impossible to explain to her that they should leave at once, walk all night if necessary. Even if he were alone, he probably wouldn't go.

Mrs Pascoe appeared at the door leading to the bar. She was carrying two glasses with steam coming from them.

'I thought you might both like a hot drink,' she said.

'Thank you,' said Phrynne. 'How nice. Oh, I think the Commandant's forgotten his book.' The book was on one of the chairs near her.

'Shall I take it up to him?' Gerald asked Mrs Pascoe. He suddenly wanted to ask the Commandant more questions.

'Thank you,' said Mrs Pascoe. 'Room One.'

When Gerald knocked on the Commandant's door, there was no reply. After the third knocking, there was still no answer, so he gently opened the door. He looked into the room and gave a little gasp.

There was no light on, but the curtains were pulled back from the open window and the noise of the bells was deafening. The Commandant was on his knees by the open window. His face was partly in his hands, but Gerald could see his expression. It seemed full of pain.

He stood watching for some time, unable to move and unable

to decide whether or not the Commandant knew he was there. Then he put the book on the bed and went quietly downstairs.

Mrs Pascoe had started drinking again. She stood near the fire, a glass of whisky in one hand.

'How long before the bells stop?' Gerald asked as soon as he came into the room. He had decided. They must go. Their excuse would be that it was impossible to sleep. 'You should have told us about this – this annual event before we booked the room.'

Mrs Pascoe drank some more whisky. 'It's not always the same night,' she said, looking at the floor.

'We're not staying,' said Gerald, wildly.

'Gerald!' said Phrynne.

'Leave this to me, Phrynne.' He turned to Mrs Pascoe. 'We'll pay for the room, of course. Please order me a car.'

'Don't go,' said Mrs Pascoe. 'Not now. It's too late.'

'Too late for what?' asked Gerald.

Her face was pale. 'You – you wanted a car. You're too late. You'll be all right if you stay. Really you will.'

Gerald put a hand on Phrynne's arm. 'Come on.'

They went first to the front door. To Gerald's surprise, it was unlocked and opened easily. Outside the building the whole sky was full of the sound of bells.

Phrynne moved close to him. 'They've been ringing too long,' she said. 'I wish they'd stop.'

'We're packing and going,' said Gerald. 'I needed to know whether or not we could get out this way.'

He tried to shut the door quietly, but it made a small noise and he hesitated with it half-shut. Suddenly, something dark and shapeless, with its arm seeming to hold a black cloth over its head, went quickly down the narrow poorly-lit street. It made

74

Gerald hesitated with the door half-shut.

no sound at all, and Gerald was very relieved that only he had seen it. With a trembling hand, he shut the door much too noisily.

Soon they were in their room with the door locked.

'Oh God!' Gerald said, dropping on to the bed. 'It's crazy out there!'

'Yes, it's crazy,' said Phrynne, almost calmly. 'And we're not going out in it.'

He did not know how much she knew, guessed, or imagined. And any explanation from him might be dangerous. He was now less frightened of the bells continuing than of them stopping.

Then one peal did stop, and Gerald sat up straight on the side of the bed. Almost at once another stopped . . . and another . . . until there was only a single bell ringing. It rang six or seven times. Then it stopped, and there was nothing.

Gerald's head was full of echoes.

Phrynne turned away from the window and started to take off her dress. 'Let's go somewhere else tomorrow.'

Sooner than usual, they were in bed and in each other's arms. Gerald had been careful not to look out of the window, and neither of them suggested opening it.

He had been afraid to look at his watch since the bells stopped, not wanting to count the hours till daylight. He could not forget the Commandant kneeling at the dark window, or the thing he had seen in the street.

Then passion drew a curtain over these memories. The old man at the window was unimportant; the street had been empty. The world was his and Phrynne's alone.

Time passed, and Phrynne lay close to him. Suddenly he heard feet moving in the road outside, and a voice calling.

'The dead are awake!'

At first Gerald lay listening, then jumped up and ran to the window. A man in a seaman's jacket was running down the street, coming into view at each street lamp. As he shouted his message, he crossed from side to side, waving his arms with joy.

'The dead are awake!'

Behind him, men, women, and children came out of their houses. Most were dressed and must have been waiting in silence and darkness for the call. Some advanced in groups, arm in arm; others ran happily, waving their arms above their heads. All cried out again and again, 'The dead are awake! The dead are awake!'

Gerald became aware of Phrynne standing behind him. 'The Commandant warned me,' he said. 'We should have gone.'

Phrynne held his arm. 'Nowhere to go,' she said. But her voice was soft with fear. 'I don't expect they'll trouble *us*.'

Quickly Gerald pulled the curtains across, leaving them in darkness. 'We'll just wait till it's over,' he said. 'It doesn't matter what happens.' He went across and pressed the light switch, but the light did not come on. 'The electricity has failed.'

He guided her back to the bed.

'They were going towards the sea,' she said nervously.

'We must think of something else,' said Gerald.

The noise was still growing. The whole town seemed to be marching round the streets, getting closer, moving away again, shouting the same dreadful words again and again. They began to shout together, like crowds at football matches, and then different words were shouted, though Gerald could not hear what they were. Finally, the shouting changed to singing, and the crowd began to approach again, slowly and steadily.

'What the *hell* are they doing now?' Gerald said.

The crowd seemed to be returning up the main street from the sea, gasping for breath, their footsteps strangely uneven. Time passed and more time.

Phrynne spoke. 'I believe they're *dancing*.'

She moved slightly, as if she thought of going to look.

'No, no,' said Gerald, and held her fiercely.

There was a huge bang from downstairs. The front door had been violently thrown open and they could hear the hotel filling with the singing crowd.

Doors banged and furniture was knocked over as the group moved through the darkness of the building. Glasses, cups and plates smashed. Phrynne screamed. Then a heavy shoulder crashed against their door and pushed it down.

The living and the dead dance together.

Now's the time. Now's the place. Now's the weather.

At last Gerald could hear the words.

Hand in hand, through the open doorway, the dancers came in, singing wildly. Happy but exhausted. More and more of them until the room must have been full.

Phrynne screamed again. 'The smell. Oh God, the smell!'

It was the smell from the beach, and here in the tightly packed room it was unspeakably horrible.

Phrynne was beyond control, screaming again and again. Gerald tried to hold her, but one of the dancers struck him so hard that she was knocked out of his arms. Instantly it seemed that she was no longer there. He struggled after her, but a huge arm knocked him to the floor, beneath the wildly dancing feet.

But soon the dancers moved on, from his room and from the building, and before long there was nothing but the darkness and the terrible smell. Unable to think or move, Gerald felt so sick that he had to battle with unconsciousness.

At last he struggled into a sitting position and put his head on the torn sheets of the bed. For a while everything went black, then he heard footsteps coming down the dark passage. The Commandant entered, holding a lighted candle.

'She's safe. No thanks to you.' He stared coldly at Gerald.

Gerald tried to stand up. He was terribly bruised, but deeply relieved to hear that Phrynne was safe.

'Is it thanks to *you*?' he asked.

'She was caught up in it. Dancing with the rest of them.' The Commandant's eyes shone brightly in the candle-light. The sound of singing and dancing had almost faded away.

Still Gerald could only sit up on the bed. 'Were they . . . were some of them . . .?'

The Commandant seemed disgusted by Gerald's weakness. 'She was between two of them. Each had one of her hands.'

Gerald could not look at him. 'What did you do?' he asked in a voice that sounded unlike his own.

'I did what had to be done. I hope I was in time.' After a slight pause he continued. 'You'll find her downstairs.'

'I'm grateful,' said Gerald.

'Can you walk?'

'I think so,' replied Gerald.

'I'll take you down.'

There were two more candles in the room downstairs. Phrynne, wearing a coat that was not hers, sat between them drinking. Mrs Pascoe moved about, collecting broken glass.

'Darling, look at you!' Phrynne's words were wild, but her voice was as gentle as usual.

Gerald pulled her into his arms. They held each other silently for a long time. Then he looked into her eyes.

'Here I am,' she said, and looked away. 'Don't worry.'

Silently and unnoticed, the Commandant had already gone.

Phrynne finished her drink, still not looking at Gerald. At the door she pulled off the coat and threw it on a chair. Her night-dress was so torn that it hardly covered her, and Gerald saw Mrs Pascoe staring with envy at Phrynne's pretty body.

'May we take one of the candles?' asked Gerald.

But Mrs Pascoe continued to stand silently staring. So they went back up through the broken furniture to their room. The Commandant's door was shut. And the smell had almost gone.

▣ ▣ ▣

Even by seven o'clock the next morning, much had been done to return everything to normal. But no one seemed to be about, and Gerald and Phrynne departed without speaking to anyone.

When they reached Station Road, they saw some men silently digging behind some gates. A sign said that it was the New Holihaven Cemetery.

In the mild light of an autumn morning, the sight of the silent workers was horrible, but Phrynne did not seem to find it so. Indeed, her cheeks reddened and for a moment her soft mouth became even more beautiful, more inviting.

She seemed to have forgotten Gerald, so that he was able to examine her closely for a moment. It was the first time he had done this since the night before. Then, once more, she became herself. But in those few seconds Gerald had become aware of something dividing them which neither of them would ever mention or ever forget.

The Stolen Body

H. G. Wells

Mr Bessel was a partner in the company Bessel, Hart, and Brown, of St Paul's Churchyard. Among those researchers concerned with the study of the mind, he was known as a very thorough investigator, but also as someone always prepared to listen to new ideas. He was unmarried and occupied rooms in the Albany, near Piccadilly. He was particularly interested in the transfer of thought and in apparitions of the living. In November 1896, he and Mr Vincent, of Staple Inn, began experiments to see if it was possible to send an apparition of themselves through space, by the power of thought.

At an arranged time, Mr Bessel shut himself in one of his rooms in the Albany and Mr Vincent in his living room in Staple Inn. Each then fixed his thoughts on the other, and Mr Bessel attempted, by the power of thought, to transfer himself as a 'living ghost' across the space of two miles to Mr Vincent's apartment. On several evenings this was tried without any satisfactory result, but on the fifth or sixth attempt, Mr Vincent did actually see or imagine he saw an apparition of Mr Bessel standing in his room. He noticed that Mr Bessel's face was white, his expression was anxious, and his hair was untidy. For a moment Mr Vincent was too surprised to speak or move, and in that moment the figure seemed to glance over its shoulder and disappear.

They had arranged to attempt to photograph any apparition,

but Mr Vincent was too slow to use the camera on the table beside him. However, excited by the first sign of success, he wrote down the exact time and at once took a taxi to the Albany to tell Mr Bessel.

He was surprised to find Mr Bessel's outside door open to the night, and lights on in the apartment. More surprising than this, a champagne bottle lay smashed on the floor, a table had been pushed over, and there were black fingermarks on the walls. One of the curtains had been torn down and thrown on to the fire and the smell of burning filled the room.

A shocked Mr Vincent hurried to the porter's house at the entrance to the Albany. 'Where is Mr Bessel?' he asked. 'Do you know that all the furniture is broken in his room?'

The porter said nothing, but came to Mr Bessel's apartment. When he saw the mess, he said, 'I didn't know about this. Mr Bessel's gone away. He's mad!'

He then explained that half an hour previously (at about the time of Mr Bessel's apparition in Mr Vincent's rooms) Mr Bessel had rushed out of the gates of the Albany into Vigo Street and disappeared in the direction of Bond Street.

'And as he went past me,' the porter said, 'he laughed, a sort of gasping laugh, with his mouth open and his eyes staring. He waved his hand, with the fingers bent like claws, and he said in a sort of fierce whisper, "*Life!*" Just that one word, "*Life!*"'

'Oh dear,' said Mr Vincent.

He waited for some time but Mr Bessel did not return. After leaving a note, he returned to his own rooms, unable to think of an explanation for Mr Bessel's behaviour. He tried to read but could not, so he went to bed early. When at last he fell into an uneasy sleep, it was at once disturbed by an upsetting dream.

He saw Mr Bessel waving his arms wildly, his face white and afraid. He even believed that he heard his friend calling to him for help. He woke up and lay trembling in the darkness. And when he finally went to sleep again, the dream returned and was even more frightening than before. He awoke with a strong feeling that Mr Bessel was in some terrible danger and needed his help. Further sleep was impossible so, although it was still dark, he got up and dressed, then went out towards Vigo Street to see if Mr Bessel had returned.

As he was going down Long Acre, something made him turn towards Covent Garden market, which was just starting to open. He heard shouting, then saw someone turn the corner and run towards him. He knew at once that it was Mr Bessel – but a much-changed Mr Bessel. He had no hat, his clothes were untidy, and his shirt collar was torn open. He held a walking-stick by the wrong end, and his mouth was pulled into a strange shape.

'Bessel!' cried Vincent.

The running man gave no sign of recognizing either Mr Vincent or his own name. Instead, he hit his friend in the face with the stick. Mr Vincent fell on to the pavement and, when he looked again, Mr Bessel had disappeared. A policeman and several market porters were running after him towards Long Acre.

Mr Vincent got up and was immediately the centre of a crowd of people, anxious to help him and to tell him about the 'madman'. He had suddenly appeared in the middle of the market screaming, '*Life! Life!*', hitting left and right with a blood-stained walking-stick, and dancing and shouting with laughter. A boy and two women had broken heads, and he had smashed a man's wrist. Next he had taken a lamp from a coffee shop and thrown it through the post office window before running away laughing.

Mr Vincent wanted to run after his friend and save him from the angry people chasing him. But then news came through the crowd that Mr Bessel had got away.

Mr Vincent returned to his rooms angry and puzzled. It seemed that Mr Bessel must have gone violently mad in the middle of the thought transfer experiment, but why did that make him appear with a sad white face in Mr Vincent's dreams?

He shut himself carefully in his room, lit his fire, washed his injured face, and tried without success to read until night became day. Only then did he go to bed and sleep.

He got up late, his bruised face in considerable pain. There was nothing about Mr Bessel in the morning newspapers and, after a visit to the Albany, where nothing had changed, he went to see Mr Hart, Mr Bessel's partner and friend.

Mr Vincent was surprised to learn that Mr Hart, although he knew nothing of what had happened to his friend, had also been disturbed by dreams of Mr Bessel, white-faced and apparently begging desperately for help.

'I was just going to go and see him at the Albany when you arrived,' said Mr Hart. 'I was sure that something was wrong with him.'

The two men decided to ask about their missing friend at the police station. Here they learned that the police had not caught Mr Bessel, but that he had gone on to smash windows along Tottenham Court Road, had hit a policeman in Hampstead Road, and had then attacked a woman.

All this happened between half past twelve and quarter to two in the morning. In fact, there was evidence of Mr Bessel's violence through London from the moment he ran from his rooms at half past nine in the evening. But after a quarter to two, when he had been seen running down towards Baker Street, he had suddenly disappeared.

All that day and all that night, Mr Vincent waited for news, but none came. In his dreams that night he again saw Mr Bessel's desperate, tear-stained face, and he also saw other faces, shadowy but evil, that seemed to be chasing Mr Bessel.

It was on the next day, Sunday, that Mr Vincent thought of Mrs Bullock, the medium, who was becoming famous in London at that time. She was staying at the house of Dr Wilson Paget.

Mr Vincent went to the house, but he had hardly mentioned the name of Bessel when Dr Paget interrupted him.

'He communicated with us last night!' said Dr Paget. 'It was at the end of the seance.'

He left the room and returned with a large piece of paper, on which were five words, written by an unsteady hand. But Mr Vincent recognised the writing. It was Mr Bessel's.

'How did you get this?' he asked.

Dr Paget explained. During the seance Mrs Bullock passed into a state of trance, during which she received a message that she wrote on the piece of paper with her left hand.

George Bessel . . . Baker Street . . . help . . .

Strangely, neither Dr Paget or the other two people who were present had heard of the disappearance of Mr Bessel. They had put the piece of paper with the many other mysterious messages that Mrs Bullock had delivered.

When Dr Paget heard Mr Vincent's story, he got to work at once to investigate this clue. And indeed, it proved to be a good clue as the missing Mr Bessel was found at the bottom of a large hole near Baker Street Station.

The hole is part of the work to prepare for the new electric railway, and it is protected by a fence nearly twenty feet high. Somehow, Mr Bessel must have climbed this fence before falling down the hole.

His arm and leg were broken, but his madness had left him. He was, of course, very weak, and when he saw his rescuers arrive, he could not stop himself crying with relief.

He was taken to a doctor's house in Baker Street and given something to help him sleep. But on the second day he gave a statement, which he has since repeated several times.

To understand it clearly, it is necessary to go back to his experiments with Mr Vincent. Mr Bessel says that he did actually, by the power of thought alone, leave his body and pass into some place or state outside this world.

'At one moment I was sitting in my chair with my eyes tightly shut,' he says, 'fiercely concentrating my mind on Vincent. Then I saw myself outside my body – saw my body near me, but not containing me. I felt I had become a kind of cloud, attached to but not part of my physical body. I could see the Albany and Piccadilly and Regent Street, and all the rooms in the houses, very small and very bright, spread out below me like a little city seen from the sky. What amazed me most is that I saw quite clearly the insides of the houses – saw people eating and drinking, talking, playing cards. I could see everything that went on.'

Those were Mr Bessel's exact words. Forgetting Mr Vincent, he remained for a time observing these things. Then, becoming curious, he reached down with a shadowy arm and attempted to touch a man walking along Vigo Street. But he could not do it, though his finger seemed to pass through the man. Something prevented him, but he finds it difficult to describe what it was. He compares it to a sheet of glass, which stopped him getting through to the physical world again. But one thing impressed him immediately. He was in a world without sound.

His first concern was where he might be. He was out of his physical body, but that was not all. He also believed that he was somewhere out of space altogether. By an enormous effort of thought, he had passed out of his body into a world beyond this world. A world not dreamed of, yet in some strange way lying so close that all things on this earth are clearly visible, both from outside and from *within*.

It was then he remembered Mr Vincent and turned his mind to travelling in this new body. For a time he was attached to his physical body, and his new strange cloud-body could not break free from it. Then quite suddenly he *was* free. For a moment everything was hidden by what seemed to be dark clouds. Then, through a break in the clouds, he saw his body fall away, and he was moving along in a strange place of shadowy clouds with London spread out beneath them.

But now he became aware that it was not clouds surrounding him, it was *faces!* Faces of thin shadow, with evil, greedy eyes and ugly smiling lips. Their cloud-like hands tried to catch him as he went past, and the rest of their bodies faded away into the darkness. No sounds came from their mouths. The shadowy Mr Bessel, now filled with terror, passed through this silent moving crowd of eyes and reaching hands.

So ghostly were these faces, so evil their staring eyes, that Mr Bessel did not think of speaking to them. Their expressions were of envy and a hungry desire for *life*.

And yet, even among these noiseless evil things, he could still think of Mr Vincent. He made a violent effort of thought and suddenly found himself moving towards Staple Inn.

Their cloud-like hands tried to catch him as he went past.

He saw Vincent sitting in his chair by the fire, and for a time he tried to get in front of his friend's eyes, to move objects in his room, to touch him. But Mr Vincent was not aware of him. That strange something that Mr Bessel compared to a sheet of glass separated them.

And at last Mr Bessel did a desperate thing. He could see not only the outside of a man but also *within*, so he reached out his shadowy hand into, it seemed, his friend's brain.

Mr Vincent sat up suddenly and in an instant Mr Bessel knew that he had been seen. At the same moment Mr Bessel knew that a great evil had happened to his body. He immediately forgot Mr Vincent and flew back to the Albany, and the countless surrounding faces flew with him, like leaves before a storm.

But he was too late. The body he had left – lying there like a dead man – had stood up, using some strength beyond his own. Now it stood with staring eyes, stretching its arms.

For a moment Mr Bessel watched, then he moved towards it. But the sheet of glass stopped him again, and the evil faces around him laughed. The little, round, middle-aged body that had once been his was now dancing with mad delight, throwing his furniture around, tearing his books, smashing bottles.

He watched all this in terrified amazement. Then, with the evil faces crowding round him, he hurried back to Vincent to tell him of the dreadful thing that had happened to him.

But the brain of Vincent was now closed against apparitions as he hurried out into Holborn to call a taxi. Defeated and full of terror, Mr Bessel again flew back to find the body he had left. It was running and shouting happily down the Burlington Arcade. It had Mr Bessel's body, but it was not Mr Bessel. It was an evil spirit out of that strange world beyond our own.

For twenty hours it held possession of Mr Bessel's body, and during that time Mr Bessel's cloud-body, or spirit, was in that mysterious middle world of shadows, looking for help. He spent many hours trying to enter the minds of Mr Vincent and of his friend Mr Hart, but without success. And all the time he was terrified that the body would be killed by its furious owner, and he would have to remain in this shadow-land for ever.

Mr Bessel was not the only human spirit in that place. He met several shadows of men like himself who had lost their bodies and who were wandering in that lost world that is neither life nor death. They could not speak because that world is silent, but he knew that they were men because of their shadowy human shapes, and the sadness of their faces.

But how had they come into that world? And where were their lost bodies? Dr Wilson Paget believes that they are the sane spirits of those men who are lost in madness on earth.

At last Mr Bessel came to a place where a little crowd of spirits was gathered. Pushing through them, he saw below a brightly lit room. In this room were four or five men, and a woman sitting awkwardly in a chair with her head thrown back. It was Mrs Bullock, the medium. And he could see a strange light – sometimes bright, sometimes faint – moving about inside her brain. She was talking, and at the same time writing with one hand. And Mr Bessel saw that the human spirits around him were all trying desperately to touch these lighted parts of her brain. When one managed to do this, or another was pushed away, her voice and her writing changed, confusing the spirit messages and making them impossible to understand. But suddenly Mr Bessel understood what was happening. The woman spoke for the spirit that touched her.

Desperately he began to struggle towards her, but he was on the outside of the crowd and could not reach her. So he went away to find out what was happening to his body.

After a long time, he found it at the bottom of a hole in Baker Street with its leg and arm broken. At once Mr Bessel returned to Mrs Bullock and the seance. It was almost finished and many of the shadows were going away in despair. Mr Bessel struggled through them and managed to reach the woman's brain. And in that moment she wrote down the message that Dr Paget kept. After that, the other shadows pushed Mr Bessel away.

He went back to Baker Street and waited, watching the evil spirit inside the body swearing and crying with pain. Then, as the night changed to day, the brain shone brightly and the evil spirit came out. And Mr Bessel entered the body he had feared he would never enter again. As he did this, the long silence ended, and he heard the traffic and the voices of people above him. And that strange world that is a shadow of our world – the dark and silent shadows of desire and the shadows of lost men – disappeared.

It was three hours before he was found in that dark, damp place, crying and in pain. But his heart was full of joy. He was back once more in the kindly world of men.

The Landlady

Roald Dahl

Billy Weaver had travelled from London on the afternoon train and by the time he got to Bath it was nine o'clock in the evening. The moon was coming up over the houses opposite the station entrance and the air was ice-cold on his cheeks.

'Excuse me,' he said, 'but is there a cheap hotel not too far away from here?'

'Try the Bell and Dragon,' the porter answered, pointing down the road.

Billy thanked him and picked up his suitcase. He was seventeen years old and had never been to Bath before, but Mr Greenslade at the Head Office in London had told him it was a beautiful city.

'Find a place to stay,' he had said, 'and then go and see the local office manager.'

There were no shops on this wide street, only a line of tall houses on each side. They had four or five steps going up to their front doors, and it was obvious they had once been very fashionable places to live. Now he could see doors and windows that needed painting, and cracks in the walls.

Suddenly, in a downstairs window that was brightly lit by a street-lamp, Billy saw a printed notice. It said: BED AND BREAKFAST. He stopped walking and moved a bit closer. Green curtains were hanging down on each side of the window. He looked through the glass into the room. On the carpet in front of the fire, a fat little dog was lying asleep. The room was filled with pleasant furniture. There was a piano, a big sofa, and several comfortable armchairs. In one corner he saw a large parrot in a cage. It seemed like a nice house to stay in.

But a pub would be more friendly, with lots of people to talk to and beer to drink. It would probably be cheaper, too. Billy decided to walk on and look at the Bell and Dragon.

He was about to turn away from the window when suddenly his eye was caught and held in the most peculiar manner by the small notice. BED AND BREAKFAST. Each word was like a large black eye staring at him, forcing him to stay where he was and not to walk away from that house. And the next thing he knew, he was actually moving across to the front door and climbing the steps that led up to it.

He pushed the bell. Far away in a back room he heard it ringing. Then *at once* – his finger was still on the bell – the door opened and a woman was standing there. She was about forty-five or fifty years old, and the moment she saw him she smiled a warm, welcoming smile.

'*Please* come in,' she said pleasantly. She held the door wide open, and Billy found that the desire to follow her into that house was extraordinarily strong.

'I saw the notice in the window,' he said, holding himself back. 'I was wondering about the room.'

'It's *all* ready for you, my dear,' she said. She had a round pink face and gentle blue eyes. 'Come in out of the cold.'

He asked the cost of the room. It was fantastically cheap.

'I would like very much to stay here,' he said.

'I knew you would,' she said. 'Do come in.'

Billy took off his hat and stepped inside.

'Just hang it there,' she said. 'And let me help you with your coat.'

There were no other hats or coats in the hall. There were no umbrellas, no walking-sticks – nothing.

'We have the house *all* to ourselves.' She smiled at him over her shoulder as she led the way upstairs. 'It's not often I have the pleasure of having a visitor in my little house.'

She's slightly mad, Billy thought, but it won't worry me at these prices. 'I'm surprised you don't get lots of people wanting to stay here,' he said politely.

'Oh, I do, my dear,' she said. 'But I'm a tiny bit fussy. I'm always ready, though, day and night, just in case an acceptable young gentleman comes along. And it's always a pleasure, my dear, when I open the door and see someone standing there who is exactly right.' She was halfway up the stairs, and she paused, turning and smiling down at him with pale lips. 'Like you,' she said, and her blue eyes travelled all the way down Billy's body to his feet, and then up again.

When they reached the first floor, she said, 'This floor is mine.' They climbed some more stairs. 'And this second floor is *all* yours. Here's your room. I do hope you like it.'

She took him into a small but pleasant front bedroom, switching on the light as she went in.

'The morning sun comes right in this window, Mr Perkins. It is Mr Perkins, isn't it?'

'No,' he said. 'It's Weaver.'

'I'm so glad you appeared,' she said. 'I was beginning to get worried.'

'That's all right,' Billy answered cheerfully. 'You mustn't worry about me.' He put his suitcase on the chair.

'Would you like some supper, my dear?' she asked.

'I'm not hungry, thank you,' he said. 'I think I'll just go to bed. Tomorrow I've got to get up early and go to the office.'

'Would you come to the living-room and sign the book? Everyone has to do that because it's the law, and we don't want to break any laws *yet*, do we?' She gave a little wave of the hand and went quickly out of the room and closed the door.

The fact that his landlady seemed to be slightly mad did not worry Billy. She was obviously a kind and generous person.

A few minutes later, after unpacking his suitcase and washing his hands, he went down to the living-room. She wasn't there, but there was the warm fire and the little dog sleeping in front of it.

He found the guest book lying open on the piano, so he took out his pen and wrote down his name and address. There were two other names above his on the page. One was Christopher Mulholland from Cardiff. The other was Gregory W. Temple from Bristol.

That's odd, he thought suddenly. Christopher Mulholland. Where had he heard that name before? He glanced down at the book again.

> *Christopher Mulholland   231 Cathedral Road, Cardiff*
> *Gregory W. Temple   27 Sycamore Drive, Bristol*

And wasn't the second name familiar, too?

'Gregory Temple?' he said aloud, searching his memory. 'Christopher Mulholland . . . ?'

'Such charming boys,' a voice behind him answered, and he turned and saw his landlady coming into the room with a large silver tea-tray in her hands.

'I'm almost sure I've heard those names before somewhere,'

he said. 'Isn't that strange? Maybe it was in the newspapers. Were they famous?'

She put the tea-tray down on the low table in front of the sofa. 'Oh no, I don't think they were famous. But they were very handsome, both of them. Tall and young and handsome, my dear, exactly like you.'

Once more, Billy glanced down at the book. He noticed the dates. 'This last entry is more than two years old. And Christopher Mulholland's entry is nearly a year before that – more than *three years* ago.'

She sighed. 'How quickly time goes by, Mr Wilkins.'

'It's Weaver,' Billy said. 'W-e-a-v-e-r.'

'Oh, of course it is!' she cried, sitting down on the sofa. 'How silly of me. I do apologize.'

'In some strange way, these two names seem to be connected,' said Billy. 'As though they were famous for the same sort of thing, if you see what I mean.'

He stood by the piano while she fussed about with cups and saucers. She had small, white, quickly moving hands, and red finger-nails.

'I'm almost sure I saw them in the newspapers,' he said. 'Wait a minute! Christopher Mulholland . . . wasn't *that* the name of the schoolboy who was on a walking-tour through the West Country, and then suddenly . . .'

'Milk?' she said. 'And sugar?'

'Yes, please. And then suddenly . . .'

'Schoolboy?' she said. 'Oh no, my dear, that can't be right because *my* Mr Mulholland was a student at Cambridge. Come over here and sit next to me and warm yourself in front of this lovely fire. Your tea's all ready for you.'

He crossed the room slowly and sat on the sofa. He drank some of his tea. She did the same. Neither of them spoke, but Billy knew that she was watching him over the edge of her teacup. A peculiar smell seemed to come from her. It was quite pleasant. What did it remind him of? New leather? Or was it the corridors of a hospital?

'Mr Mulholland enjoyed his tea,' she said. 'I have never seen anyone drink as much tea as Mr Mulholland.'

'I suppose he left fairly recently,' Billy said.

'Left?' she said. 'My dear boy, he never left. He's still here. Mr Temple is also here. They're on the third floor, both of them together.'

Billy put down his cup slowly and stared at his landlady.

She smiled back at him. 'How old are you, my dear?'

'Seventeen,' he said.

'The perfect age!' she cried. 'Mr Mulholland was also seventeen, but he was a little shorter than you are, and his teeth weren't *quite* so white. Mr Temple was twenty-eight. And yet his skin was just like a baby's.'

There was a pause. Billy drank some more of his tea and stared at the corner of the room. 'That parrot,' he said at last. 'You know something? When I first saw it through the window from the street, I was convinced it was alive.'

'I'm afraid not,' she said.

'It's very clever, the way it's been done,' he said. 'It doesn't look at all dead. Who did it?'

'I did.'

'*You* did?'

'Of course,' she said. 'And have you met my little Basil as well?' She nodded towards the little dog lying so comfortably

Billy touched the dog gently on the top of its back.

by the sofa. Billy looked down at it. And suddenly he realized that the animal had been just as silent and still as the parrot. He put out his hand and touched it gently on the top of its back. The back was hard and cold, and when he pushed the hair to one side with his fingers, he could see the skin underneath. It was a grey-black colour, dry and perfectly preserved.

'How absolutely fascinating,' he said. He turned admiringly to the little woman on the sofa beside him. 'It must be awfully difficult to do something like that.'

'Not in the least difficult,' she said. 'I preserve *all* my little pets when they die. Will you have another cup of tea?'

'No, thank you,' Billy said. The tea tasted faintly bitter, and he didn't like it very much.

'You did sign the book, didn't you?' she said.

'Oh, yes.'

'That's good. If I forget your name later on, then I can always look in the book. I still do that almost every day with Mr Mulholland and Mr . . . Mr . . .'

'Temple,' Billy said. 'Gregory Temple. Excuse my asking, but haven't there been any *other* guests here except them in the last two or three years?'

Holding her teacup high in one hand, she looked up at him out of the corners of her eyes and gave him another gentle little smile.

'No, my dear,' she said. 'Only you.'

Laura

Saki

'You are not really dying, are you?' asked Amanda.

'I have the doctor's permission to live till Tuesday,' said Laura.

'But today is Saturday!' gasped Laura. 'This is serious!'

'I don't know about it being serious; it is certainly Saturday,' said Laura.

'Death is always serious,' said Amanda.

'I never said I was going to die. I suppose I'm going to stop being Laura, but I shall go on being *something*. Some kind of animal, I suppose. You see, when a person hasn't been very good in their life, they reincarnate in some lower form of creature. And I haven't been very good, when I think about it. I've been mean, and sometimes cruel and unforgiving, when circumstances seemed to demand it.'

'Circumstances never demand that sort of thing,' said Amanda quickly.

'If you don't mind my saying so, my cousin Egbert is a circumstance that would demand a large amount of that sort of thing,' said Laura. 'You're married to him, and you've promised to love and obey him. I haven't.'

'What's wrong with Egbert?' protested Amanda.

'Oh, it's probably me who has been wrong,' admitted Laura coolly. 'Egbert has just been the excuse for my bad behaviour. He made a bad-tempered fuss the other day, for example, when I took the young dogs from the farm out for a run.'

'They chased his young chickens and ran all over the flowers in his garden. You know how he loves his chickens and his garden.'

'Anyway, he didn't have to complain about it for the whole of the evening and then say, "Let's say no more about it" when I was beginning to enjoy the discussion.' Laura smiled. 'So I had my revenge and allowed all his chickens to get into his garden shed and eat his seeds.'

'Oh!' cried Amanda. 'And we thought it was an accident!'

'So you see,' Laura continued, 'I really do have reasons for supposing that I shall be some lower form of creature when I am reincarnated. I shall be an animal of some kind. But I think I shall be a nice animal, something handsome and with a love of fun. An otter, perhaps.'

'I can't imagine you as an otter,' said Amanda.

'Well, I don't suppose you can imagine me as an angel, either,' said Laura.

Amanda was silent. She couldn't.

'Actually, I think life as an otter would be quite enjoyable,' continued Laura. 'And then, if I'm quite a good otter, I suppose I should get back into a human shape of some sort. Nothing too grand – a little brown, unclothed Nubian boy, I should think.'

'I wish you would be serious,' sighed Amanda. 'You really ought to be if you're only going to live till Tuesday.'

In fact, Laura died on Monday.

'It's so upsetting,' Amanda complained to her husband's uncle, Sir Lulworth Quayne. 'I've asked quite a lot of people to come and stay, to play golf and go fishing. And the gardens are looking so beautiful now.'

'Laura was always thoughtless,' said Sir Lulworth.

'She had the craziest kind of ideas,' said Amanda. 'Was there any insanity on her side of the family, do you know?'

'Insanity? No, I never heard of any. Her father lives in West Kensington, but apart from that I believe he's quite sane.'

'She had an idea that she was going to be reincarnated as an otter,' said Amanda.

'These ideas of reincarnation are quite common, even in the West,' said Sir Lulworth. 'They can't really be considered mad. And Laura was such a surprising person in this life, I shouldn't even like to guess what she might be doing in the next one.'

'Do you really think she might have become some sort of animal?' asked Amanda. She was one of those people who readily adopt other people's opinions.

Just then Egbert entered, looking extremely unhappy; far too unhappy for Laura's death to be the reason.

'Four of my best chickens have been killed,' he said. 'One of them was pulled right into the middle of my new flower garden and was eaten there! The flowers are ruined!' Egbert looked ready to cry. 'My best flower garden and my best chickens! It's almost as if the horrible creature that did it *knew* this.'

'What sort of creature—?' began Amanda.

'There were footmarks to and from the stream at the bottom of the garden,' said Egbert. 'It must have been an otter.'

Amanda looked quickly and secretly at Sir Lulworth.

Egbert was too upset to eat any breakfast. He went outside to make stronger fences around the chicken houses.

'I think she might at least have waited until after the funeral,' said Amanda in a shocked voice.

'It's her own funeral, you know,' said Sir Lulworth. 'Why should she be polite about it?'

While the family were attending the funeral the next day, the last of Egbert's chickens were killed. And the killer's escape route seemed to have taken in most of the flowerbeds, and the strawberry beds in the lower garden.

'I shall get the otter hounds to come and hunt for this creature as soon as possible,' said Egbert, angrily.

'Oh, but you can't!' exclaimed Amanda. 'It's not polite, so soon after a funeral.'

'It has to be done,' said Egbert. 'Once an otter starts this sort of thing, it won't stop.'

'Perhaps it will go somewhere else now that there are no more chickens left,' suggested Amanda.

'I'm beginning to think you want to protect the creature,' said Egbert.

'There's been so little water in the stream lately,' said Amanda. 'It doesn't seem very sporting to hunt an animal when it has so little chance of escaping anywhere.'

'I'm not thinking about *sport*,' shouted Egbert. 'I want to have the animal killed as soon as possible.'

Even Amanda found it difficult to continue to argue in the otter's defence when, during church time on Sunday, it got into the house and found half a salmon, then tore it into pieces on the carpet in Egbert's study.

'We shall have it under our beds and biting pieces out of our feet soon,' said Egbert, and from what Amanda knew about this particular otter she felt that was quite possible.

On the evening before the hunt, Amanda walked alone by the stream for an hour, making what she imagined to be hound noises. Those people who heard her decided kindly that she was practising animal imitations for the next village entertainment.

It was her friend and neighbour, Aurora Burret, who brought her news of the day's sport.

'We had quite a good day,' Aurora said. 'We found the otter at once, in the pool just below your garden.'

'Did you . . . kill . . .?' asked Amanda.

'Of course. A fine she-otter. Your husband got rather badly bitten trying to cut off its tail. Poor creature. I felt quite sorry for it. It had such a human look in its eyes when it was killed. You'll say I'm silly, but do you know who the look reminded me of? My dear, what's the matter?'

Some days later, when Amanda recovered from her nervous attack, Egbert took her to the Nile Valley. The change of scenery soon improved her health, and she returned to her usual relaxed and peaceful state, able to remember the otter's adventures quite calmly. Even hearing her husband swearing angrily in his dressing room in the Cairo hotel did not upset her.

'What's the matter? What has happened?' she called, amused.

'The little devil has thrown all my clean shirts into the bath!' shouted Egbert. 'Wait until I catch you, you little—!'

'What little devil?' asked Amanda, trying not to laugh.

'A little devil of a naked brown Nubian boy,' said Egbert.

And now Amanda is seriously ill.

GLOSSARY

ahoy a cry used by people on boats to attract attention

alibi the proof that you were elsewhere when a crime happened

angel a spirit who is believed to be a messenger of God, often
shown as a creature with wings

apparition an image of a person who is not present

ashtray a container for cigarette ends and ash

asylum a hospital where people who are mentally ill are cared for

atom a very small particle of matter

barbecue an outdoor meal where food is cooked on an open fire

booth a small enclosed space where you can do something
privately (e.g. make a telephone call in a phone booth)

brass a bright yellow metal made of copper and zinc

cabin a small room, often on a ship

cathedral a large, important church; the main church of a district

cemetery a piece of land where dead people are buried

champagne an expensive French white wine with bubbles in it

chef a professional cook

confirm to say or show that something is definitely true

conveyor (line) a moving surface used to carry things from one
place to another

courtyard an open space enclosed by the walls of buildings

crew all the people working on a ship, an aeroplane, etc.

deck the top outside floor of a ship or boat

disc a thin flat circular object

dip to put something quickly into a liquid and take it out again

disintegration the process of breaking into small pieces

dome a round roof with a circular base

faith a strong religious belief

fungus   a soft furry plant that grows on decaying matter

gallery   a high platform on the inner wall of a church, hall, etc.

guillotine   a machine with a sharp blade, used for cutting people's heads off

guinea pig   a small animal with short ears and no tail, often kept as a pet

honeymoon   a holiday taken by a newly married couple

hounds   dogs used for hunting

insurance   money paid to protect yourself against the cost of a possible disaster

landlady   a woman from whom you rent a room or a house

mast   a tall pole on a boat that supports the sails

medium   a person who says they can communicate with the spirits of dead people

monster   an unnatural creature that is ugly and frightening

motel   a hotel for people travelling by car, with space for car parking near the rooms

oar   a long pole with a flat blade at one end, used to move a boat through water

otter   a small animal with thick brown fur that lives in rivers

parrot   a brightly coloured tropical bird with a curved beak

peal   (of bells) to ring loudly

porter   a person in charge of the entrance to a large building

raft   a flat structure made of pieces of wood tied together and used as a boat

reincarnate   to be born again in another body after you die

saint   a person recognized as very holy by the Christian church

salmon   a large fish with pink flesh

sane   not mad (the opposite is **insane**)

schooner   a sailing ship with two or more masts

seance a meeting at which people try to make contact with the spirits of dead people

set to make a machine ready for use

shed a small building used to store tools, wood, bicycles, etc. or to shelter animals

skeleton the bones that support the body of a person or animal

spider a small creature with eight thin legs

strawberry a small red juicy soft fruit

stick (past tense **stuck**) to become fixed to something with a sticky substance

suck to take liquid into your mouth by using the muscles of your lips

sweat liquid that appears on your skin when you are very hot or ill

tar a thick black sticky liquid used in making roads

temple a building used for religious purposes

tile a flat square piece of baked clay, used for covering walls, etc.

trance a state in which you appear to be asleep but are aware of things around you

transmit to send signals (electronic, radio, TV, etc.) through the air

tray a flat board for carrying cups and plates

velvet a thick soft expensive fabric

verger a person whose job is to look after the inside of a church

web a structure of fine threads made by a spider to catch insects

Before Reading

1 Read the back cover, and the story introduction on the first page of the book. What do you expect to find in these stories? Would you agree with these statements about horror stories?

   1 The best horror stories always have something supernatural in them: dead bodies, ghosts and spirits, monsters, and so on.
   2 Horror stories can have happy endings.
   3 Horror stories can make you laugh.
   4 Horror stories can contain quite ordinary, natural events; what makes them horror stories is the way they are written.
   5 Horror stories are most effective when the 'horror' is only suggested, and is not described in detail.

2 Here are a number of ideas that might or might not appear in the first story, *The Fly*. How do they affect you? Give each one your own 'horror rating' of 1 to 5 (5 for the most horrible).

   1 A scientist invents a machine that turns flies into creatures as big as human beings.
   2 A scientist creates flies as big as dogs, which he trains to work as his servants.
   3 In a deliberate experiment a scientist turns his wife into a fly; he then keeps her, as a fly, in a box for the rest of her life.
   4 In an experiment that goes wrong, a scientist becomes part man, part fly; the mistake cannot be undone and he kills himself.
   5 An army of giant flies escapes from a laboratory and starts to kill humans and animals.

While Reading

Read *The Fly*, to the bottom of page 11. What will happen to these three characters? Choose as many answers as you like.

Hélène / François / Commissaire Charas will . . .

1 kill himself / herself
2 be killed
3 go mad
4 read / not read the confession
5 believe / not believe the confession
6 destroy the confession

Read *Cooking the Books*, to the bottom of page 33. How do you think the story will end? Choose from these possibilities.

If the restaurant burns down, . . .

1 will Haldeman get the insurance money?
2 will Hyatt guess what happened and blackmail Haldeman?
3 will Haldeman get arrested for murder?

If there is no gas explosion, . . .

4 will Hyatt still telephone Haldeman at the motel as arranged?
5 will Haldeman die in an accident before he learns what has happened?
6 will Haldeman try his plan again a few days later?

Read *A Voice in the Night*, to the bottom of page 42. Can you guess the answer to this question?

Where are the people from the ship now?

1 On the ship
2 On the shore
3 On the ship and the shore
4 At the bottom of the sea

Now read to the end of *A Voice in the Night*. Can you explain the importance of these sentences in the story?

1 'I am only an old . . . man.' p37
2 'We had much to learn.' p42
3 '. . . the decks were covered in more of the grey fungus, some of it in shapes about two metres high.' p42
4 'We were, all at once, afraid of something worse than death.' p45
5 'And in that dreadful ending I had seen our own.' p48

Read *The Whispering Gallery*, to the bottom of page 59. How do you think the story ends?

1 Jim and Mrs Stagg arrive in time to rescue Frederic.
2 Frederic's experience is so frightening that he dies of shock.
3 St Paul rescues Frederic from the Death figure and carries him away; Frederic is never seen again.
4 Frederic jumps from the gallery and dies when he hits the floor.

Now read to the end of *The Whispering Gallery* and answer these questions.

1 What does Frederic understand about voices, and what does he not understand about size and distance?
2 What kind of child is Frederic, and how would you describe his relationship with his mother?
3 The golden ball belongs to the 'light' side of the story, and Skeleton-face to the 'dark' side. What other things and ideas from the story belong to each side?
4 How does the second verger explain the voice that calls 'Way!'?

Read *Ringing the Changes*. Does the story answer these questions? If not, what answers can you think of from your own imagination?

Why do the people of Holihaven wake the dead each year?
The Commandant 'knows what to do' on the night. What is that, and how does he know it?
What does Phrynne do while she is separated from Gerald?
What is it that now divides Gerald and Phrynne?

Read *The Stolen Body*, to the bottom of page 89. How do you think the story continues? Choose from these ideas.

Mr Bessel follows his own body around London and eventually drives the evil spirit out by the power of thought.
The evil spirit leaves Mr Bessel's body when the body becomes damaged and causes the evil spirit to feel pain.
Mr Bessel regains his own body, but in fact the evil spirit has not left and Mr Bessel becomes a kind of split personality, one day sane, the next day mad.

Read *The Landlady* and answer these questions.

What do you think happened before Billy arrived at the house?
What do you think is going to happen next?
What are the clues in the story that make you think this?
At what point in the story did you guess the ending?

Read *Laura* and answer this question.

Why do you think Amanda falls seriously ill at the end of the story?

ACTIVITIES

After Reading

1 **Perhaps this is what some of the characters in the stories were thinking. Which eight characters are they (one from each story), and what has just happened in the story at this moment?**

1 'There – he has it now. Soon he will know everything. I hope he uses his knowledge wisely. He says he will come and see me tomorrow, after he has read it. But he won't see me. No. It's time to make an end now . . .'

2 'I've got to – oh, let me through! I must get a message to somebody before they stop. I've got to touch her brain – if I push a bit harder . . . yes! I'm there, she's writing . . .'

3 'I hope this isn't going to take too long. Why ever did he want to come here? What strange ideas children get! Where are we going now? Oh, the underground rooms. Well, if we must . . .'

4 'Suppose it really *is* her. Surely it can't be. Oh, I just don't know what to think. But I can't bear to think of the hounds tearing her to pieces. I've been walking up and down for an hour now, so perhaps she'll realize I'm trying to warn her . . .'

5 'That's done, then. I'd better find him and take him to her. The man's a fool, though. Why didn't he take her away when I told him to? He's going to regret that for a long time . . .'

6 'He's down by the sea fishing, so he won't see me. I'll just have a little bit more. It tastes good, I like it, it tastes sweet . . . I don't want to eat it, but I'm so hungry – so, so hungry . . .'

7 'He's perfect – just perfect. It's been such a long time, but he's come at last. Such beautiful teeth too. I think he deserves the silver teapot – it's a special day for both of us.'

8 'That's very strange – there's no answer. He insisted I should ring at exactly three o'clock. Let's see – yes, it's the number he gave me. Well, I'll just have to try again in a few minutes.'

2 **Complete this conversation between Commissaire Charas and François. Use as many words as you like.**

COMMISSAIRE CHARAS: So you think your sister-in-law was telling the truth, do you?

FRANÇOIS: ＿＿＿＿＿＿

COMMISSAIRE CHARAS: What makes you so sure it's not just a crazy story invented by a madwoman?

FRANÇOIS: ＿＿＿＿＿＿

COMMISSAIRE CHARAS: Even sensible people can change, you know, and sometimes quite suddenly.

FRANÇOIS: ＿＿＿＿＿＿

COMMISSAIRE CHARAS: Perhaps she drugged him, and then put him there herself.

FRANÇOIS: ＿＿＿＿＿＿

COMMISSAIRE CHARAS: Then perhaps he was the crazy one, and she agreed to end his suffering. I don't think we'll ever know the answer – because this story is just too awful to believe.

FRANÇOIS: ＿＿＿＿＿＿

COMMISSAIRE CHARAS: Do? I'm not going to do anything. The case is closed. Let us hope that these two poor souls are now at peace.

3 Here are some different titles, two for each story. Which titles go with which story, and in each pair, which is the most obvious title, and which the less obvious? Decide which titles you prefer and why, and then think of another title for each story.

The Fungus People	Just Come This Way . . .
Lost and Found	Boiled to Death
Room to Rent	The Golden Ball
The Life of an Atom	Honeymoon in Hell
Permanent Resident	A Deadly Hunger
Revenge Beyond the Grave	A Sticky End
Head Under the Hammer	Dancing with Death
Mr Bessel's Narrow Escape	Reincarnation

4 Here are two newspaper reports about Frederic's death and Mr Bessel's adventure. Decide which sentences go in which report. Put the parts of sentences in the right order, and use these linking words to join the sentences and make two paragraphs. (Begin with number 5 for one report, and number 11 for the other.)

after / after which / and / and then / before / in spite of / that / where / while / who

1 _____ he could do anything to stop him, however,

2 _____ was breaking windows and attacking people.

3 _____ he attacked a policeman and a woman.

4 _____ walked to the cathedral alone.

5 Police were called to St Paul's Cathedral yesterday evening

6 _____ ran through Covent Garden Market,

7 Verger Nathaniel Hill told police

8 _____ police investigated the death.

9 _____ a long search of the Baker Street area,

114

10 It seems that Frederic left the hotel room

11 In central London last night police spent several hours chasing a dangerous man

12 screaming, *'Life! Life!'*

13 _____ he saw the boy standing on the rail of the gallery.

14 police were unable to find him.

15 _____ he was staying with his mother

16 The man first damaged his apartment in the Albany,

17 _____ five-year-old Frederic Stagg fell to his death from the Whispering Gallery.

18 He was later seen smashing windows in Tottenham Court Road,

19 the child appeared to jump off the rail.

20 The cathedral was closed last night for three hours

5 **At the end of *Ringing the Changes*, what do you think happens next? Choose one of these ideas (or think of one of your own) and write a new ending for the story.**

- Phrynne refuses to talk / Gerald can't forget / one day Phrynne gone / Gerald returns to Holihaven / Commandant says forget her / leaving, Gerald sees her – or does he?

- Phrynne troubled by Holihaven memory / one day confesses all to Gerald / sell story to newspaper / make a lot of money . . .

- Year later / Phrynne persuades Gerald to return / get rid of memories / bells ring / events repeat themselves / Phrynne sinks teeth into Gerald's neck . . .

How did you feel about the horror in these stories? Give each story a score from 1 (hardly scary) to 10 (truly frightening). Then choose three of your favourites. Write a short paragraph about each one recommending it to a friend, but without giving away the story.

ABOUT THE AUTHORS

ROBERT AICKMAN
Robert Aickman (1914–1981) was born in London. He worked as a critic and then became an expert in the field of supernatural short fiction. He edited eight collections of ghost stories and published nine collections of his own short stories, which often feature women at a crucial moment in their lives.

ROALD DAHL
Roald Dahl (1916–1990) was born in Wales of Norwegian parents. His collections of short stories, *Someone Like You*, *Kiss Kiss*, and *Tales of the Unexpected* have become bestsellers all over the world. His storytelling is skilful, bizarre, and disturbing. His children's books are also very popular.

CHRISTOPHER FOWLER
Christopher Fowler (1953–) lives and works in London, where he is the director of The Creative Company, a film production organization. A fan of horror, fantasy and science-fiction writing since his schooldays, he began writing in the 1980s. His novels include *Roofworld*, *Red Bride*, *Spanky*, and *Psychoville*, and he has been called 'the finest author working in horror today'.

WILLIAM HOPE HODGSON
Hodgson (1877–1918) was born in Essex. After eight years in the Merchant Navy, he ran a school of physical culture, then turned to writing, specializing in horror stories featuring monstrous life-forms such as slime, fungus, rot, and giant rats. 'The Voice in the Night' is his most famous short story. He was killed in action in the First World War.

GEORGE LANGELAAN

George Langelaan (1908–1969) was born in France, but has British nationality. He has published novels and short stories in both English and French, but by far his most famous work is 'The Fly', published in 1957. It has been widely translated and filmed twice, once in 1958 starring Vincent Price, and also in 1988.

SAKI

Hector Hugh Munro (1870–1916), the British writer known as Saki, was born in Burma and grew up in England. He became a successful journalist, working in Paris, Poland and Russia, and is best known for his short stories, which are both cruel and funny. He published five collections of short stories and two novels. Saki was killed in France during the First World War.

WILLIAM F. TEMPLE

Temple (1914–1989) was born in London, and worked in the London Stock Exchange. He became friendly with such notable science-fiction writers as Arthur C. Clarke and John Wyndham, and wrote several novels and many short stories. In his writing he is as interested in personalities and the inner world of the mind as he is in the science-fiction scenery he creates for his characters.

H. G. WELLS

Hubert George Wells (1866–1946) worked as a teacher and a journalist before achieving fame through writing. Novels such as *The Time Machine* (1895) and *The War of the Worlds* (1898) marked the beginning of what we know as science fiction; more than a hundred years later his novels still excite interest, as shown by a recent filming of *The Time Machine*.

OXFORD BOOKWORMS LIBRARY

Classics • Crime & Mystery • Factfiles • Fantasy & Horror
Human Interest • Playscripts • Thriller & Adventure
True Stories • World Stories

The OXFORD BOOKWORMS LIBRARY provides enjoyable reading in English, with a wide range of classic and modern fiction, non-fiction, and plays. It includes original and adapted texts in seven carefully graded language stages, which take learners from beginner to advanced level. An overview is given on the next pages.

All Stage 1 titles are available as audio recordings, as well as over eighty other titles from Starter to Stage 6. All Starters and many titles at Stages 1 to 4 are specially recommended for younger learners. Every Bookworm is illustrated, and Starters and Factfiles have full-colour illustrations.

The OXFORD BOOKWORMS LIBRARY also offers extensive support. Each book contains an introduction to the story, notes about the author, a glossary, and activities. Additional resources include tests and worksheets, and answers for these and for the activities in the books. There is advice on running a class library, using audio recordings, and the many ways of using Oxford Bookworms in reading programmes. Resource materials are available on the website <www.oup.com/bookworms>.

The *Oxford Bookworms Collection* is a series for advanced learners. It consists of volumes of short stories by well-known authors, both classic and modern. Texts are not abridged or adapted in any way, but carefully selected to be accessible to the advanced student.

You can find details and a full list of titles in the *Oxford Bookworms Library Catalogue* and *Oxford English Language Teaching Catalogues*, and on the website <www.oup.com/bookworms>.

THE OXFORD BOOKWORMS LIBRARY
GRADING AND SAMPLE EXTRACTS

STARTER • 250 HEADWORDS

present simple – present continuous – imperative –
can/cannot, must – *going to* (future) – simple gerunds ...

Her phone is ringing – but where is it?

Sally gets out of bed and looks in her bag. No phone. She looks under the bed. No phone. Then she looks behind the door. There is her phone. Sally picks up her phone and answers it. *Sally's Phone*

STAGE 1 • 400 HEADWORDS

... past simple – coordination with *and, but, or* –
subordination with *before, after, when, because, so* ...

I knew him in Persia. He was a famous builder and I worked with him there. For a time I was his friend, but not for long. When he came to Paris, I came after him – I wanted to watch him. He was a very clever, very dangerous man. *The Phantom of the Opera*

STAGE 2 • 700 HEADWORDS

... present perfect – *will* (future) – *(don't) have to, must not, could* – comparison of adjectives – simple *if* clauses – past continuous – tag questions – *ask/tell* + infinitive ...

While I was writing these words in my diary, I decided what to do. I must try to escape. I shall try to get down the wall outside. The window is high above the ground, but I have to try. I shall take some of the gold with me – if I escape, perhaps it will be helpful later. *Dracula*

STAGE 3 • 1000 HEADWORDS

... should, may – present perfect continuous – *used to* – past perfect –
causative – relative clauses – indirect statements ...

Of course, it was most important that no one should see
Colin, Mary, or Dickon entering the secret garden. So Colin
gave orders to the gardeners that they must all keep away
from that part of the garden in future. ***The Secret Garden***

STAGE 4 • 1400 HEADWORDS

*... past perfect continuous – passive (simple forms) –
would* conditional clauses – indirect questions –
relatives with *where/when* – gerunds after prepositions/phrases ...

I was glad. Now Hyde could not show his face to the world
again. If he did, every honest man in London would be proud
to report him to the police. ***Dr Jekyll and Mr Hyde***

STAGE 5 • 1800 HEADWORDS

... future continuous – future perfect –
passive (modals, continuous forms) –
would have conditional clauses – modals + perfect infinitive ...

If he had spoken Estella's name, I would have hit him. I was so
angry with him, and so depressed about my future, that I could
not eat the breakfast. Instead I went straight to the old house.
Great Expectations

STAGE 6 • 2500 HEADWORDS

... passive (infinitives, gerunds) – advanced modal meanings –
clauses of concession, condition

When I stepped up to the piano, I was confident. It was as if I
knew that the prodigy side of me really did exist. And when I
started to play, I was so caught up in how lovely I looked that
I didn't worry how I would sound. ***The Joy Luck Club***